SEEDTIME AND HARVEST

Unraveling the Foundational Principle of God's Kingdom

JOSEPH OLOWE

Seedtime and Harvest

Unraveling the Foundational Principle of God's Kingdom

Copyright © 2019 by **Joeseph Olowe**
ISBN: 978-1-944652-89-0

Printed in the United States of America. All rights reserved solely by the publisher. This book or parts thereof may not be reproduced in any form, stored in a retrieval system, or transmitted in any form by any means - electronic, mechanical, photocopy. Unless otherwise noted, Bible quotations are taken from the Holy Bible, New King James Version. Copyright 1982 by Thomas Nelson, Inc., publishers. Used by permission.

Published By:
Cornerstone Publishing
A division of Cornerstone Creativity Group LLC
Info@thecornerstonepublishers.com
www.thecornerstonepublishers.com

Author's Information

To contact the author or to order copies of the book:

8700 Montana Avenue,
El Paso Texas 79925

1-800-561-9170 or +1 915-478-8807
www.drjosepholowe.com | info@drjosepholowe.com

CONTENTS

Dedication..7
Acknowledgments..9
Introduction..11

1. A Parable Like No Other....................................13
2. To Reap, We Must Sow.......................................25
3. Seeds That Never Grow......................................55
4. Seeds With Aborted Growth..............................75
5. Preparing For A Bountiful Harvest....................89
6. Your Heart And Your Harvest..........................111
7. Sure Ways To Build Up Your Faith..................125
8. Open The Eyes Of My Heart............................131
9. Your Harvest, Your Hands And Your Feet.......141

About The Author..149

DEDICATION

To my dad and mom, Mr Hezekiah Aremu Olowe and Deaconess Felicia Aduke Olowe - both now late - who showed me the way of the Lord in my early years. The seed you sowed in us has blossomed into these mighty revelations.

To my parents-in-law, the late Pastor Israel Omotosho Ayeni and Deaconess Beatrice Amope Ayeni, whose many seeds of ceaseless prayers led to this great outpouring of knowledge to the body of Christ. My wife and I will be forever grateful for showing us the way to Calvary.

ACKNOWLEDGMENTS

I would like to appreciate my Savior, Jesus Christ, from whom all blessings flow. My sincere gratitude to my wife and partner in ministry, Omolade, for her relentless pursuit of excellence for our family first and the ministry.

I thank my children, Olamide, Simi and Dare, who have given me an opportunity to practice what I am preaching.

To my ministry team, first to my able editor who I consider as a gift from heaven to me, Pastor Joseph Ola and to Daniel Emonido who I refer to as mighty Danny, for all the divine graphics; many thanks. To Pastor Gbenga Showunmi and his professional team at Cornerstone Publishing, thank you for making this dream come true.

To a good friend of mine, Pastor David Olayemi — the first man apart from my family, who sincerely believed in my writing gift and encouraged me to pursue my dream — may the God of heaven never forget your labor of love.

INTRODUCTION

It is with great joy that I introduce you to a book that is about to revolutionize your life with the truth of God's Word. The principle unpacked in this book—Seedtime and Harvest—is perhaps the most popular and arguably most misapplied principle in all of the canon of scriptures. We live in a dispensation when the mention of the word "seed" in the mouth of evangelical preachers is almost synonymous with "money". We hear today of the prosperity gospel that seems to have overtaken a large expression of the Christian faith, both in such developed countries as the United States and even in third world countries where the Christian faith is booming exponentially. Yet, this seedtime-harvest principle is principal to our appropriation of all that God has to offer us as His children. Hence, our need to have a good grasp of it.

With our work of redemption completed and perfected in Jesus, our potential and privileges as Christians are immense! Yet, we are so easily prone to limitations through our sight and our human reasoning that the devil never stops bombarding us with the agents of such limitation. This book was written so that we may know the enemy's strategies and how to overcome them. This we shall do by unpacking this transformational principle called "Seedtime and Harvest".

We will learn how not to put our trust in our sight and human reasoning, but to use the spiritual weapons available to us to our advantage and to have a richer understanding of how the Kingdom of God works, so that we can enjoy the 'FULL CORN' thereof. This book's main aim is to broaden our understanding of how the Kingdom into which we have been redeemed works. And as we undertake the journey to unravel the messages that God has specifically given to us through the seedtime and harvest principles, I assure you that something new, remarkable, unforgettable and life-changing is about to manifest in all aspects of your life!

1
A PARABLE LIKE NO OTHER

And He said to them, "Do you not understand this parable? How then will you understand all the parables? (Mark 4:13)

The parable of the sower, which is the classic manual on the "seedtime and harvest" principle, is not only one of the most popular but also one of the most profound parables in the Scripture. In itself, this parable is deeply insightful, enriching and empowering; but when examined alongside the parable of the growing seed, as we will be doing shortly, what you get is a treasure chest of revelations that are sure to catapult you to a newer and greater dimension of dominion and impact in every area of your life.

However, before we unlock the contents of this chest, we need to understand a few truths about it and especially why it is vitally important that we give it absolute attention. Let us begin by recalling that a scriptural parable is an earthly narrative with a heavenly meaning. This means that a parable, especially one coming from the Lord Himself, is not just a story to delight or even teach a moral lesson, but a revelation of weighty divine truths that are deliberately encrypted in a seemingly earthly narrative.

On the surface, a parable would seem like an easy-to-understand illustration, since it primarily uses day-to-day realities and imageries. Yet this is not always the case; often hidden beneath the images used in a parable are layers of truth about life in general and God's Kingdom in particular that need to be carefully unraveled to get the hidden messages. In Matthew 13:35, Jesus, quoting from Isaiah, reveals the content of parables, "I will open my mouth in parables; I will utter what has been hidden since the foundation of the world."

Did you notice that? Parables contain truths that have been hidden to many from the foundation of the world. The primary purpose of truth is to emancipate, invigorate and elevate (John 8:32). This means that for anyone who can rightly and fully discern the hidden contents of parables, they are bound to live with such understanding and function at such a realm of power and impact that is unprecedented – which is exactly where God desires you to be!

So, Why Hide Truths in Parables?

This is a natural question to ask. Jesus Christ taught a lot in parables. Indeed, there are about 52 of His parables recorded in the Scripture; and Matthew 13:34 specifically says, "All these things Jesus spoke to the multitude in parables; and without a parable He did not speak to them." So, what is the purpose of these allusions if their interpretations are not always on the surface?

While parables are often used to make heavenly messages more realistic and practical to us, they have a deeper purpose, which Christ Himself reveals in Matthew 13:10-13, "And the disciples came and said to Him, "Why do You speak to them in parables?" He answered and said to them, "Because it has been given to you to know the mysteries of the kingdom of heaven…Therefore I speak to them in parables, because seeing they do not see, and hearing they do not hear, nor do they understand."

What this simply means is that parables are a veritable means of determining and separating sincere seekers of God and His Kingdom from the insincere and the half-hearted. Parables contain veiled truths, which sincere seekers painstakingly do all they can to uncover, while the insincere simply either focus on the literal meaning or decide not to bother at all about the meaning.

Therefore, in seeking to unravel the truths hidden in the parables of the sower and of the growing seed, we are positioning ourselves as bona fide recipients of life-changing truths that have been hidden from many from the foundations of the world. Praise God!

KEY TO ALL KINGDOM MYSTERIES

Here is another vital reason we are paying particular attention to the parable of the sower. It is a foundational parable - because the principle of "sowing and reaping" or "seedtime and harvest" which it contains provides the key to unlocking the meanings embedded in all other parables. This, by extension, means that if we do not have proper understanding of the place and power of this principle, then many mysteries of the Kingdom cannot be unraveled by us. Jesus told the disciples when they asked Him for the interpretation of the parable of the sower, "Know ye not this parable? and how then will ye know all parables?" (Mark 4:13).

Does Jesus imply here that this parable is the easiest to understand of all His parables and thus shouldn't have been a problem to the disciples? Not at all. Rather, as I will be illustrating shortly, it points to the centrality of this parable to understanding life in God's Kingdom. Charles Ellicott, in his commentary on this verse says, "The question is peculiar to St. Mark, and suggests the thought of our Lord as contemplating for His disciples an ever-growing insight, not only into His own spoken parables, but into those of nature and of life. But if they were such slow scholars in this early stage, how was that insight to be imparted?" Johann Bengel, on his part, says "Jesus marks with reproof the question of the disciples. The parable concerning the seed is the primary and fundamental one [the foundation of all the others] — constituting and comprising the perfect doctrine of Christ."

It goes without saying then that the reason many believers continue to fall short of certain blessings that God expects us to have is because we do not have the understanding we ought to have concerning this foundational principle of seedtime and harvest. Let me break it down for you. Christ, by that seemingly simple question, clearly reveals that the sowing and reaping principle governs the universe as a whole, holds a central place in God's Kingdom and helps significantly to extract the messages hidden in Christ's other parables.

APPLICATION TO LIFE

There is no doubt that understanding the parable of the sower will helps us understand other parables told by Christ because each of them contains elements of the principle of sowing and reaping. However, since parables are meant to help us to understand life and the Kingdom better, let me get down to more specific realities of day-to-day life in the Kingdom and unearth proofs from the Scripture that they contain elements of seedtime and harvest. I have highlighted six areas of life here and the scriptural evidence that they are connected to the sowing and reaping principle.

1. **Marriage.** God says the basic purpose of marriage is to raise godly seeds - which definitely involves sowing and reaping. "And did not he make one? Yet had he the residue of the spirit. And wherefore one? That he might seek a godly seed…" (Malachi 2:15). How do you raise seeds without sowing? No way. Therefore, if marriage involves raising seeds, then definitely some understanding of seedtime and harvest is indispensable!

2. **Family life and child-raising.** As with marriage, the imagery of plants is used in describing family life and raising of children in the believer's home. Psalm 128:3 says, "Thy wife shall be as a fruitful vine by the sides of thine house: thy children like olive plants round about thy table." I need not go into extensive explanation to show that a fruitful vine growing by the sides of a house or olive trees around a table require the same principles and skills that an experienced farmer needs! Again, Psalm 144:12 says, "That our sons may be as plants grown up in their youth…"

3. **Enjoying financial and material blessings.** The level of material and financial blessings a believer enjoys is intrinsically linked to his or her understanding and application of the seedtime and harvest principle. 2 Corinthians 9:6-8 says, "But this I say, He which soweth sparingly shall reap also sparingly; and he which soweth bountifully shall reap also bountifully. Every man according as he purposeth in his heart, so let him give; not grudgingly, or of necessity: for God loveth a cheerful giver. And God is able to make all grace abound toward you; that ye, always having all sufficiency in all things, may abound to every good work."

4. **Evangelistic and ministerial success.** Achieving success in our evangelistic and ministerial efforts require that we are familiar with the principle and process involved in sowing and reaping, as well as the place and significance of the personalities involved. Paul wrote to the Corinthians, "I have planted, Apollos watered; but God gave the increase. So then neither is he that planteth any thing, neither he that watereth; but God that giveth the increase. Now he that planteth and he that watereth are one: and every man shall receive his own reward according to his own labour" (1 Corinthians 3:6-8). Earlier on, the Psalmist had given the assurance,

"They that sow in tears shall reap in joy. He that goeth forth and weepeth, bearing precious seed, shall doubtless come again with rejoicing, bringing his sheaves with him" (Psalm 126:5-6).

You may wonder why such graphic allusions have to be made to the painful, laborious and patient process of planting and harvesting, when the intended message is the process and reward of soul-winning (or any other applicable area of life). The reason is simple – we must see that there is a close connection between this natural principle and the Kingdom life!

5. **Personal and congregational revival.** The process of experiencing revival, whether in our individual lives or in our churches is, as the Scripture reveals, closely linked to the seedtime and harvest principle. This was why Prophet Hosea declared to the Jewish nation, "Sow to yourselves in righteousness, reap in mercy; break up your fallow ground: for it is time to seek the LORD, till he come and rain righteousness upon you" (Hosea 10:12).

6. **Educational, career and business pursuits.** As with the other areas of life and ministry that I have already pointed out, making a success of our academic, professional and entrepreneurial aspirations requires a fundamental understanding

of seedtime and harvest. The reason is because we go through the same routines as the farmer – and if we don't know the process by which sowing and harvesting works, then we may linger longer in the valley of expectation and procrastination. The Scripture counsels, "He who observes the wind will not sow, and he who regards the clouds will not reap. As you do not know what is the way of the wind, Or how the bones grow in the womb of her who is with child, So you do not know the works of God who makes everything. In the morning sow your seed, And in the evening do not withhold your hand; For you do not know which will prosper, Either this or that, Or whether both alike will be good" (Ecclesiastes 11:4-6).

There are other areas of life concerning which the scripture shows us a clear connection with seedtime and harvest. But I believe that with the above, you should have received a better understanding of why Jesus had to ask that phenomenal question, "Know ye not this parable? and how then will ye know all parables?" I pray the Holy Spirit further illuminate your spirit to fully grasp the power and import of the message that the Lord is revealing to us here.

DIMENSIONS OF DISCOVERY

Now that we have established a solid background for our exploration of the amazing seedtime and harvest principle, we have a brief layout of the approach we shall be taking in enjoying its benefits. Let's do this by recounting the parable of the sower, alongside the parable of the growing seed, as told by our Lord:

"Hearken; Behold, there went out a sower to sow: And it came to pass, as he sowed, some fell by the way side, and the fowls of the air came and devoured it up. And some fell on stony ground, where it had not much earth; and immediately it sprang up, because it had no depth of earth: But when the sun was up, it was scorched; and because it had no root, it withered away. And some fell among thorns, and the thorns grew up, and choked it, and it yielded no fruit. And other fell on good ground, and did yield fruit that sprang up and increased; and brought forth, some thirty, and some sixty, and some an hundred. And he said unto them, He that hath ears to hear, let him hear…

And he said, So is the kingdom of God, as if a man should cast seed into the ground; And should sleep, and rise night and day, and the seed should spring and grow up, he knoweth not how. For the earth bringeth forth fruit of herself; first the blade, then the ear, after that the full corn in the ear. But when the fruit is brought forth, immediately he putteth in the sickle, because the harvest is come." (Mark 4:3-9, 26-29).

From the literal narration, highlights of these parables include:

- Seed-sowing
- Death of some seeds before germination
- Termination of growth of some seeds after germination
- Certainty of fruit-bearing by some seeds, in various degrees
- Process of the growth and fruit-bearing stages.

Now, we are set – let's unpack this treasure chest of blessings and soar to the next level of dominion!

CLOSING THOUGHT

"And he said unto them, Unto you it is given to know the mystery of the kingdom of God…" (Mark 4:11)

It is indeed a great privilege we have to be able to access and understand the mysteries of God's Kingdom. This understanding comes only as we spend quality time studying and meditating on the word, while depending on the Spirit of God to give us the best interpretation applicable to our situation. This requires a heart that is open, attentive and receptive to God's word. How often do you read God's word and how seriously do you take its messages? Are you a sincere or an insincere seeker?

CALL TO ACTION

Prepare a schedule to prayerfully study each of the parables of Jesus, with the aim of ascertaining the hidden meanings in them.

PRAYER POINTS

1. Father, give me a heart that sincerely seeks after you.

2. Lord, fill me with a deep hunger and thirst for your word daily.

3. Lord, give me special insights into the mysteries of your Kingdom.

4. Father, let the entrance of your word into my life fill me with understanding and illumination.

5. Lord, cause your word to prosper and accomplish its purpose in all areas of my life

2

TO REAP, WE MUST SOW

"Hearken; Behold, there went out a sower to sow... So is the kingdom of God, as if a man should cast seed into the ground." (Mark 4:3,26)

God created the whole universe in six days and rested on the seventh. He made man in His image—creating both male and female—and He made them the object of His love. He gave them His blessings and a dominion mandate. As the story continued, man sinned and the plan of redemption was activated immediately.

By the time we get to Genesis chapter 6, we are introduced to a man called Noah. Noah was a righteous man chosen by God to carry out a key part of this redemption assignment. After forty days of constant rain, the earth was destroyed and the plan to re-create was set in motion by an interesting process revealed to us in Genesis 8:22: "While the earth remaineth, seedtime and harvest, and cold and heat, and summer and winter, and day and night shall not cease."

By implication, we are made to understand that the process by which this earth realm functions involves seeding and harvesting.

The devil understands this and he's actively seeking for ways to hinder us from knowing and understanding this principle. For instance, when he tempted Jesus in the wilderness by asking Him to turn stones to bread, notice the response Jesus gave him.

"And when the tempter came to him, he said, If thou be the Son of God, command that these stones be made bread. But he answered and said, It is written, Man shall not live by bread alone, but by every word that proceedeth out of the mouth of God." (Matthew 4:3-4)

In a sense, the devil wanted Jesus to substitute His seed for bread. Seed is for the sower and it guarantees a potential for harvest while bread is for the eater (and once it is eaten, that's the end of it). Hence, Apostle Paul wrote: "God gives seed to the farmer and food to those who need to eat." (2 Corinthians 9:10, GW)

PURPOSE OF GOD'S DECLARATION

Let's return to God's declaration concerning seedtime and harvest in Genesis 8. While this was originally intended to assure Noah and the other remnants of the earth that normalcy would soon return to the earth and that the earth would never be destroyed by a flood again, the pronouncement has a deeper meaning for us – to harvest, we must sow.

Let me put this in another way. That message was a way of God telling you and me that even though many things had been swept away by the flood and a new generation of mankind was to inhabit the earth, the core principles that had been laid by God from the foundations of the earth must continue unabated – one of which is the seedtime and harvest principle. In other words, flood or no flood, as long as the earth remains, seedtime must precede harvest. We must sow if we expect to reap!

Now, you must understand – especially from the various areas of life that we outline in the previous chapter - that this sowing and harvesting does not necessarily have to do with putting agricultural seeds in the ground and ultimately harvesting the corresponding crops. Not at all. It is not about the particular words or imageries employed but the principle behind it. God was simply saying there was no other way that the earth was going to be able to function without this principle – nor was there going to be any other way that humans would be able to fulfill the mandate of dominion given to us by God over the earth. In other words, to be fruitful, to multiply and to have dominion over the earth, we must realize that seed-sowing must never and can never cease!

I don't find it surprising that God had to reestablish or rather re-emphasize this principle to Noah. It was the way He created the earth and all that is in it, in the first place; that is to say it was the foundation on which the earth itself was laid. Yes, it was by sowing that the harvest of all the beauties of nature and the inhabitants of the earth manifested. What do I mean by this and, more importantly, how does it apply to you? Let me show you.

The Bible says this concerning the creation of the earth and all that we see in it: "In the beginning God created the heaven and the earth. And the earth was without form, and void; and darkness was upon the face of the deep. And the Spirit of God moved upon the face of the waters. And God said, Let there be light: and there was light" (Genesis 1:1-3).

Here, we are not exactly told the way God created the earth, but we are told of how he CONFIGURED it – by sowing the seed of the WORD. It is interesting that after God had made the earth, He found it to be shapeless, empty and full of darkness; in other words, the earth did not come "pre-loaded" or ready-made. God had to bend it to shape, illuminate it and fill it up by sowing the seed of the word into it. God needed to reap the harvest of a beautiful world that suited His desires and purpose, and He had to sow something into it – the power of the word.

I don't know if you are getting the message here already. But if you haven't, let me make it plain – words are SEEDS and they have the power to produce an abundant harvest of fruits, depending on their contents. God Himself confirms this by making us know that His words are seeds that have infinite, catalyzing capabilities. "For as the rain cometh down, and the snow from heaven, and returneth not thither, but watereth the earth, and maketh it bring forth and bud, that it may give seed to the sower, and bread to the eater: So shall my word be that goeth forth out of my mouth: it shall not return unto me void, but it shall accomplish that which I please, and it shall prosper in the thing whereto I sent it." (Isaiah 55:10-11)

Indeed, from that time of creation, when God configured the world with His words, He has been remolding lives and destinies, uprooting mountains and limitations, breaking yokes and curses, making ways where there were none, as well as causing unlimited provisions and breakthroughs by sowing the seed of His words. I tell you today that if you would let God speak into your spirit, soul, body and mind, impossibilities will become possibilities for you, sickness and disease will give way to health and vitality, negative reports and diagnoses will be cancelled and every work of darkness in your life will be banished. No wonder that when Jesus wanted to visit the home of the centurion whose servant was sick, the centurion simply told Him, "Speak the word only, and my servant shall be healed." (Matthew 8:8)

YOU HAVE SAME SEED

Now, this is even more interesting. The power to reap a harvest of wonders with words is not restricted to God. Being His representatives on earth, we have been vested with the same power to shape our worlds and determine the course of our destinies and those of the people connected to us. Here is how God tells us that our words are seeds – "Death and life are in the power of the tongue: and they that love it shall eat the FRUIT thereof" (Proverbs 18:21).

Fruits come from seed. So there's no mistaking what God is saying here. You can consciously sow the seed of life or the seed of death through the word of your mouth. You can, like God, decide what you wish to see in existence and what you would like to be exterminated by the words of your mouth.

Jesus Christ, in fact, not only declared that we have this power and authority but also went ahead to demonstrate how it works. In Matthew 18:18, He says, "Verily I say unto you, Whatsoever ye shall bind on earth shall be bound in heaven: and whatsoever ye shall loose on earth shall be loosed in heaven." I like the way someone describes this "binding and loosing". According to him, "In usage, to bind and to loose simply means to forbid by an indisputable authority and to permit by an indisputable authority." It means that with the words of our mouth, we can choose what to permit or forbid in our lives, homes, communities, churches and nations.

I will shortly be illustrating what I mean by this "forbidding and permitting", using scriptural examples. But let me first refer to Christ's demonstration on the subject. You know, being the greatest teacher who ever lived, Christ always taught with compelling wisdom and practical demonstration. And so, soon after revealing the power the disciples had to bind and to lose, he showed them exactly what He meant. Matthew 21:17-21 narrates: "And he left them, and went out of the city into Bethany; and he lodged there. Now in the morning as he returned into the city, he hungered. And when he saw a fig tree in the way, he came to it, and found nothing thereon, but leaves only, and said unto it, Let no fruit grow on thee henceforward for ever. And presently the fig tree withered away. And when the disciples saw it, they marvelled, saying, How soon is the fig tree withered away! Jesus answered and said unto them, Verily I say unto you, If ye have faith, and doubt not, ye shall not only do this which is done to the fig tree, but also if ye shall say unto this mountain, Be thou removed, and be thou cast into the sea; it shall be done."

You would think that with all the assurances, examples and demonstrations that we have on the creative power of the spoken word, Christians should be taking charge of their world, shaping the lives of their children, transforming the lives of others and directing the course of events in their communities and nations by deliberately sowing the words of their mouth. But what we see most of the time are Christians who are cringing before demons, cowering under sicknesses, lamenting about the state of things around them and generally allowing evil and darkness to prevail.

We cannot go on this way. Every believer is an embodiment of power and authority. Our words, as members of the family of the King of Kings, are active activators and we must make optimum use of them. Ecclesiastes 8:4 says, "Where the word of a king is, there is power…" We must realize who we are and what we have – otherwise, the meaninglessness, emptiness and darkness that seem to hover over our lives, homes and destinies will persist.

Things remained bleak and gloomy on the earth, until God sowed the seed of the word. I tell you, there are many mountains, yokes and situations that we are battling with currently that only waiting for us to declare, "be thou removed" – and if we don't sow this seed, we may not get the harvest of miracles and breakthroughs that we eagerly desire. If we do not sow, we cannot expect to reap!

Luke 21:15 says, something inspiring, "For I will give you a mouth and wisdom, which all your adversaries shall not be able to gainsay nor resist." This is a conversation that Jesus had with His disciples. Jesus promised to give them two weapons to use against the adversary: their mouth and godly wisdom (which comes from The Word). Jesus did not talk about faith, hope or patience in this instance, but "a mouth". Why? Because lying inside our mouth is our tongue! It is with this tongue in our mouth that we set the course of our lives.

God's way of rousing Prophet Ezekiel to this consciousness of the power of the believer's word is particularly enlightening. Ezekiel had been led to see the miserable and seemingly hopeless state of the Israelites, represented by a valley full of withered and scattered bones. And when God asked him if he thought anything could be done about the situation, he did what most of us often do – he said it was all up to God to decide. But God basically reminded him of his role as a prophet: "Prophesy upon these bones…" (Ezekiel 37:4). And of course, as Ezekiel prophesied, "there was a noise, and behold a shaking, and the bones came together, bone to his bone…and the breath came into them, and they lived, and stood up upon their feet, an exceeding great army" (7-10).

How many areas of our lives are like this valley of dry bones and we are busy waiting for God to do something! Truth is, in most cases, God has done all that needs to be done – He has given us the mandate to sow our words into our lives and the lives of others (using the name of Jesus) and consequently reap the harvest of healing, deliverance and breakthrough. Jesus says, "these signs shall follow them that believe; In my name shall they cast out devils" (Mark 16:17).

What else do we need? See, God will not do for us what we have been empowered to do for ourselves. Let's take a cue from champions of faith like Joshua, who commanded the sun and the moon to stand still, so that the Israelites could obtain total victory over their enemies. It might interest you to know that he did not first spend hours in prayer or even ask God to "come and take control" – instead, he sowed the seed of the word and the result was a resounding and historic victory.

SOWING THE WORD INTO OTHERS' LIVES

The Scripture says of our heavenly Father, "He sent his word, and healed them, and delivered them from their destructions." (Psalm 107:20). So we know that not only did God use the seed of the word to create the earth, but He has also been using the word to cause healing and deliverance for successive generations of mankind. And this is what we must do also. Our words are not only meant to bring transformations and testimonies to our lives – but they must also be actively sown into the lives of others. This could be all that they need for salvation, healing, guidance and deliverance.

Many people who have given in to depression or committed suicide might have been saved, if they had heard the right words at the right time. Prophet Isaiah said of the seed he had and what he was doing with it, "The Lord GOD hath given me the tongue of the learned, that I should know how to speak a word in season to him that is weary." (Isaiah 50:4)

We all have been given this seed and we can greatly enrich and enhance people's lives with it. But, first, this "charity" must begin from our very homes. If we want the harvest of a happy home, we must learn to sow the seed of sweet, courteous, gracious, complimentary and (when necessary) apologetic words into the lives of our spouses daily. It is because many of us refuse to sow this seed that we don't reap the harvest of peace and joy that we expect. Again, to reap, we must sow!

It is the same with our children. Right from the womb, we must begin to sow the seed of the word of life into their lives. We must begin to prophesy upon them, shaping them into the kind of children we want them to be. And after they are born, the seed of teaching, prophesying, affirmation and advice must continue to be sown into them, so as to guide them aright in life. It is said of Timothy and what made his life to be one of distinction, "And that from a child thou hast known the holy scriptures, which are able to make thee wise unto salvation through faith which is in Christ Jesus" (2 Timothy 3:14).

Outside our home, we must consciously reach out to others with the seed of the gospel. The harvest of righteousness that we expect to see in our communities is not appearing because we are not even sowing the required seed of the word. All over the world, and especially in Western countries like the USA and

Britain, we continue to receive the alarming reports about Christianity shrinking and churches being converted to pubs and mosques. This is most times because many churches have stopped sowing the seed of the word. The church began with the seed of the gospel, and only this seed can sustain it.

There cannot be conversion of souls without the seed of the word being continually sown into people's lives everywhere. Paul the apostle says in Romans 1:16, "For I am not ashamed of the gospel of Christ: for it is the POWER of God unto salvation to every one that believeth…" (Emphasis mine). He says again in Romans 10:13-14, "For whosoever shall call upon the name of the Lord shall be saved. How then shall they call on him in whom they have not believed? and how shall they believe in him of whom they have not heard? and how shall they hear without a preacher?"

Sometimes, the complaint is that people are rejecting or ridiculing the message of the gospel that we are presenting to them. But we must remember that it is not our job to covert people or pull them into the Kingdom; our job is simply to SOW the seed of the word and water it – while God takes care of the rest. Here's Apostle Paul again, " I have planted, Apollos watered; but God gave the increase. So then neither is he that planteth any thing, neither he that watereth; but God that giveth the increase. Now he that planteth and he that watereth are one: and every man shall receive his own reward according to his own labor" (1 Corinthians 1:6-8).

This same seed of the word must be sown into the lives of our employees, subordinates, clients and customers. In communication studies, this is an aspect of what is called "public relations." You don't have to wait for a crisis to happen before saying positive and complimentary things about the people who are in one way or the other connected to your business. Sow words of appreciation, motivation and understanding as much as possible, into their lives, and you will be surprised by the harvest of goodwill you will get from these different categories of people in the long run.

WORDS SOMETIMES REQUIRE ACTION

So far, we have taken our time to consider ways in which we can sow the seed of our words to bring about the harvest of wonders that we expect to see in every area of our lives. Sometimes, however, words alone will not do; we must sow, together with our words, decisive actions that will help to actualize the harvest that we expect. I will show you, from the Scripture, the different ways in which this works. And it should come as no surprise that our first port of call again will have to be the Almighty God Himself.

Recall that when discussing words as seed, we referred to God as using the seed of the word to bring light, order, purpose and fullness to the darkness, chaos and emptiness that initially characterized the earth. But then, here is something really interesting. After God had sown the word for five consecutive days and harvested the various outcomes he anticipated, it was soon time to create man – the crown of His creations. For this however, God went beyond words and went into action: "And the Lord God formed man of the dust of the ground, and breathed into his nostrils the breath of life; and man became a living soul.

And the Lord God planted a garden eastward in Eden; and there he put the man whom he had formed." (Genesis 2:7-8). Two things I want you to observe here. One since man was to be a special creation, he had to be specially "formed", not just called forth. The second thing I want you to see is that God consciously planted a garden. Why would God plant a garden, when He had already called forth plants? This again, is to tell you that there are some harvests you cannot get by merely sowing words. There is a difference between a man and a beast; and there is a difference between a plant and a garden. A garden, as my dictionary tells me, is "a plot of ground where herbs, fruits, flowers, or vegetables are cultivated." And thus, in creating the man, as well as in creating a garden, God had to go into strategic action, using what had already been made.

What revelations are you getting from the above exposition? There are times you bring certain things into existence by simply sowing words of faith. As I mentioned earlier, when Joshua was to halt the movement of the sun and the moon, all he had to do was declare (or sow) the word. But then, there are times you make things happen by combining words with action. When Peter and John ministered deliverance to the cripple at the Beautiful Gate, they first sowed the seed of the word – "Then Peter said, Silver and gold have I none; but such as I have give I thee: In the name of Jesus Christ of Nazareth rise up and walk"; thereafter, they sowed the action, "And he took him by the right hand, and lifted him up: and immediately his feet and ankle bones received strength" (Acts 3:6-7). And there are times when you reap your harvest by simply creatively using or sowing what has already been created in you, for you or around you – as God has shown us in the above example. What this means is that the harvest of miracles that we sometimes wait for donkey years to get without seeing is simply around the corner, waiting for us to sow the seed of innovative thinking, methodical planning and strategic action.

PRACTICAL APPLICATIONS

When the children of Israel were being pursued by the Egyptians on their way out of Egypt, all they could do was lament and regret in in their camp which was close to the Red Sea. Moses, on his part, was busy sowing the seed of the word of faith and encouragement to calm their nerves, saying: "Fear ye not, stand still, and see the salvation of the Lord, which he will shew to you to day: for the Egyptians whom ye have seen to day, ye shall see them again no more for ever. The Lord shall fight for you, and ye shall hold your peace." (Exodus 14:13).

But God told Moses, neither their wailing nor his declaration was what was needed at that point in time. What was needed for their victory was ACTION! Even if He would fight for them as Moses believed, they still needed to act and Moses himself needed to use what he had been given. "And the Lord said unto Moses, Wherefore criest thou unto me? speak unto the children of Israel, that they go forward: But lift thou up thy rod, and stretch out thine hand over the sea, and divide it: and the children of Israel shall go on dry ground through the midst of the sea." (15-16).

You see, dear reader, it is of utmost importance that we understand this aspect of sowing because it appears to be a major area of challenge for many believers.

Believers have, by default, been blessed with the seeds of a sound mind (full of creativity) and inborn talents. But many times we just do not think enough to apply these seeds. No wonder, Jesus Christ says, "…for the children of this world are in their generation wiser than the children of light" (Luke 16:8).

There are times when we complain of financial lack, hardship or lack of opportunities – when, God has, in fact, given us the seed that we need to sow to reap our harvest of blessings. There are talents and gifts that we have been given to give us unprecedented breakthroughs, but most times we refuse to sow these natural endowments. There are skills which we have acquired but never put to use – because we are not sure whether we will succeed or not. Instead, we keep making professions of faith, while remaining at the same level.

Consider the example of Isaac. He was a child of promise, no doubt. Moreover, his father, Abraham, had been a very wealthy man and the blessing of the father was sure to flow to the son. But the prosperity that Isaac needed did not come magically or by his declaration of himself as the seed of Abraham. Rather, it came by his taking the decisive action of sowing, which we can in present times call investing. "Then Isaac sowed in that land, and received in the same year an hundredfold: and the Lord blessed him. And the man waxed great, and went forward, and grew until he became very great" (Genesis 26:12-13).

Let's get even more practical with the seed of action. Take your spiritual life, for instance. See, you cannot merely continue to declare that "I'm growing by grace and getting stronger everyday" - without taking the necessary spiritual food of regular study of God's word, communion with God and fellowship with fellow believers. That's what you must sow to get the yield of strength and growth that you want.

How about the student who wants to master a difficult subject or excel above his peers? What of the job-seeker who wants to get the lucrative employment in a highly competitive environment? Or the professional who wants to be outstanding in his field? Or the employee who wants promotion? Or the businessman who wants customer loyalty and all-round expansion? Do these just wait on God, while making positive declarations? No way. The uniform testimony of God's word is: "Seest thou a man diligent in his business, he shall stand before kings and not before mean men." (Proverbs 22:29).

The student must sow the seed of extra diligence and inquisitiveness; the job-seeker must work on his qualifications, resume, interview skills, as well as positioning himself as someone ready to be an asset, not a liability to any prospective organization. The professional can never be tired of sowing in researches and being abreast and (possibly) ahead of developments in his field. The employee must be seen as a paragon of excellence in competence and character; while the businessman must go the extra mile in providing value-added products and services, in addition to ensuring good customer and staff relationship. These are seeds that must be sown if we must reap.

What of marriage, family life and child-raising? There are decisive steps that we must take to keep our marriages blissful, peace and exciting. It is not just by assuming that being Christians, then all must naturally go smoothly. To keep reaping, we must keep sowing. We must invest in applying scriptural principles for strengthening the home. We must invest in marriage books and seminars, sowing the seed of going the extra mile to understand the preferences of our spouses and making them happy. It will also take taking decisive actions to safeguard the home from physical and spiritual invaders.

In terms of child training, we cannot expect to raise children grown in their youth or as cornerstones polished after the similitude of a palace without consciously sowing the actions of spending quality time to be with them, attending to their needs, playing with them, answering their questions and disciplining them.

This should partly provide an answer to the question that many often ask as to why children of believers or even church leaders sometime turn out to be wayward or rebellious. The truth is that we need more than mere teaching and prophetic pronouncements. This was where Eli failed. He wanted children who could deputize for him in the holy calling, but the seed of firmness of action and discipline that he needed to sow into their lives wasn't there. He wanted to reap the harvest of godly and responsible children, but he wasn't ready to sow the necessary seed. Even when God called his attention to this, all he could say was, "It is the Lord: let him do what seemeth him good." (1 Samuel 3:18).

On the opposite but very positive side, I don't know if you have read the remarkable success story of Ben Carson as a student and later as a globally-acclaimed neurosurgeon. How did he get there? It was the seed of action sown into his life as a child. You may have heard of how, at one time, he was considered the dullest and "dumbest" student in his class. Of course, his mother, Sonya, gave him lots of motivational talks and affirmations. And she also prayed. But according to Ben, what really brought the much needed transformation to his life was when his mother took the drastic action of turning off the television. Here is his testimony:

My mother couldn't stand the fact that we were doing poorly in school, and she prayed and she asked God to give her wisdom. What could she do to get her young sons to understand the importance of developing their minds so that they control their own lives? God gave her the wisdom. At least in her opinion. My brother and I didn't think it was that wise. Turn off the TV, let us watch only two or three TV programs during the week. And with all that spare time read two books a piece from the Detroit Public Libraries and submit to her written book reports, which she couldn't read but we didn't know that.

I just hated this. My friends were out having a good time. Her friends would criticize her. My mother didn't care. But after a while I actually began to enjoy reading those books. Because we were very poor, but between the covers of those books I could go anywhere. I could be anybody. I could do anything. I began to read about people of great accomplishment. And as I read those stories, I began to see a connecting thread. I began to see that the person who has the most to do with you, and what happens to you in life, is you...

That is what sowing the seeds of right actions could produce in the life of a child. If we want extraordinary children, then we must take actions to sow the appropriate seed into their lives.

MINISTRY AND KINGDOM EXPANSION

Now, let's come to the ministry and Kingdom expansion. It is not uncommon to hear church leaders and workers continually talk of church growth; but the irony is that many do not want to go through the process and rigor of church planting. We simply prefer to stay in, perhaps, one comfortable location and remain there for eternity. How can there be church growth without church planting? What is God going to bless if we do not make the effort to plant? Where we read earlier, Apostle Paul says, "I have planted, Apollos watered; but God gave the increase." (1 Corinthians 3:6).

How do we think Jesus was able to reach multitudes of souls with the word within the three years that He ministered? He was not just settled in a place, sowing the seed of the word; he was taking necessary actions by moving from place to place. Here is a typical example in Mark 1:35-38, "And in the morning, rising up a great while before day, he went out, and departed into a solitary place, and there prayed. And Simon and they that were with him followed after him. And when they had found him, they said unto him, All men seek for thee. And he said unto them, Let us go into the next towns, that I may preach there also: for therefore came I forth."

Right there is a powerful secret of church growth and Kingdom expansion! Jesus had just been told that His ministry was fast becoming popular in a particular town and that everyone was eager to see Him. This is a sign of success and He should have just listened to what people were saying and remained in that comfort zone. Yet, He swiftly replied that he must continue to move into other towns, so the word could be sown. If we cannot follow this example, we cannot get the harvest of souls we are expecting or the transformation we are expecting to see in our nations.

Moreover, keeping our churches free of pollution, worldliness and backsliding will go beyond sowing the seed of the word on every service day. There are times when we need to sow the seed of decisive actions, so we can reap the harvest of untainted righteousness and decorum that the church requires. Paul wrote thus to the Corinthians, "It is reported commonly that there is fornication among you, and such fornication as is not so much as named among the Gentiles, that one should have his father's wife. And ye are puffed up, and have not rather mourned, that he that hath done this deed might be taken away from among you… Your glorying is not good. Know ye not that a little leaven leaveneth the whole lump? Purge out therefore the old leaven, that ye may be a new lump, as ye are unleavened. For even Christ our passover is sacrificed for us" (1 Corinthians 5:1-7).

There are several other areas of our lives in which sowing the seed of action is as important as sowing our words, but I'll summarize it this way. We cannot claim to love – whether God or our fellow men – without backing our words with actions. John 3:16 says that God says loved the world that He "GAVE." It was the Seed He gave that has continued to bring salvation, hope and deliverance to humanity. In return, Christ says. "If ye love me, keep my commandments…" If we truly love God and expect to reap blessings, then we must sow the seeds of love into His Kingdom, not just by words but also by actions. We must give our time, talents and resources towards the advancement of the Kingdom.

Moreover, we cannot claim to love brethren in the church or our fellow men, with sowing the seeds of kindness and our resources into their lives. It is as we sow mercy and kindness in practical ways that we shall reap. Proverbs 19:17 says, "He who has pity on the poor lends to the Lord,

And He will pay back what he has given."Our gifts are seeds and we shall reap abundant harvests. So, if we want to reap mercy and favor, we must sow same into the lives of others.

In our health too, we must sow the actions of checking what we eat, going for routine checkups and doing necessary exercise – it is not just by sowing seeds of words of faith; we must sow the right actions!

ATTITUDE AND ALTITUDE

The saying, "attitude determines altitude" may have become a cliché – but it is nonetheless true and must be taken seriously in the context of sowing and reaping. We get from life what we sow and expect from it. As it is said in the world of computing, "garbage in, garbage out." To get the best from life, you must continually sow the right attitude into it. You cannot continue to sow the wrong attitude into life – believing that you are a victim, a failure or a loser – and not find yourself reaping harvests of failures and frustration. When the disciples of Jesus asked him why they could not perform a certain miracle, He told them, "because of your unbelief". You cannot sow the seeds of a loser into life and expect to reap the harvest of a champion.

Once again, to reap, we must sow. If you want the harvest of positive experiences in life, then you must sow the seed of positive expectations. If you want to see unprecedented possibilities in your life, then you must continually sow the seeds of anti-impossibility mindset. As you go out each morning, begin to sow the seeds of great expectations of unlimited favor and mercies. The Psalmist says, "This is the day that the Lord has made, we will rejoice and be glad in it." Every day dawns with freshness of divine mercies. And it is in your best interest that you sow into the day the seeds of expectation of these mercies to be your portion.

A man is what he thinks he is (Proverbs 23:7). This is why Henry Ford said, "Whether you think you can or cannot, you are right." You must believe that, as a child of God, anything is possible and surmountable; and you will find yourself exceeding expectations and achieving what others find impossible. You must believe that you are fearfully and wonderfully made. You cannot continually sow the seed of such positive mindset and reap the harvest of inferiority complex or low self-esteem.

The reason the Israelites reaped the harvests of failure and destruction on their way to Canaan was because they had the attitudes of failures. They saw themselves as nothing but grasshoppers and they ended up dying as grasshoppers. They had a "problem" mentality, which made them to always see adversity in every opportunity. But Joshua and Caleb who chose to sow the seed of positivity received the harvest of conquests and possession. Theirs was a "solution" mentality; thus they saw opportunity in seeming adversity and faced their challenges with this mindset. The result was historic triumph.

Sowing the right attitude also has to do with our relationship with others. Proverbs 18:24 says, "A man that hath friends must shew himself friendly…" To attract an atmosphere of love, peace, joy and harmony in our homes, community, workplaces, schools and churches, we need not wait for others to do good to us; rather, we must sow the exact attitude that we wish to see in the lives of others – and we will reap a bountiful harvest all around.

Once again, I must remind you. To reap, we must sow. What harvest do you intend to reap in your life, home, church, workplace and community today, this week, this month or this year? Whatever it is, don't just wish and hope. Let the sowing begin and keep it going!

CALL TO ACTION

Outline areas of your life where you need to sow and list the kind of seed you will sow into each. Then, begin the sowing right away!

CLOSING THOUGHT

"They that sow in tears shall reap in joy. He that goeth forth and weepeth, bearing precious seed, shall doubtless come again with rejoicing, bringing his sheaves with him." (Psalm 126:5-6)

The process of sowing, in practical terms, is not always easy. This is why the above Scripture adds "tears" and "weeping" to it. But, then, as the same passage reveals, the reward is always worth the effort. So, whatever area of life in which you expect a harvest, you must begin today to take the right step of sowing – speak the word, take action, and demonstrate the right attitude always. Soon, you will have cause to rejoice.

PRAYER POINTS

1. Father, I thank you for the power of the world with which you created and transformed the word.

2. Father, I thank you because the creative and re-creative power of your word remains forever.

3. Lord, I pray that you speak your word to calm every storm in my life, subdue every mountain and make every crooked path straight in my life.

4. Lord, help me to speak the right words, take the right actions and demonstrate the right attitude that will bring about the changes I expect to see in my life.

5. I declare healing, strength, health, vitality, progress, prosperity and open doors in all areas of my life in Jesus' name.

3

SEEDS THAT NEVER GROW

"And it came to pass, as he sowed, some fell by the way side, and the fowls of the air came and devoured it up." (Mark 4:4)

We have indeed had an enriching and enlightening time exploring the importance and necessity of seed-sowing. And of course, it is natural for you to want to start spreading your seeds as far and wide as possible. But wait a minute – there is something vital that you must know. It is not all seeds sown that germinate, much less come to maturity or produce the expected harvest. You may have noticed this yourself and, perhaps, started to wonder why this is so. Why do we sow the seed of the word, actions and attitude and we don't get the commensurate reward?

Jesus Christ, in explaining the seed that fell by the wayside, says, "And these are they by the way side, where the word is sown; but when they have heard, Satan cometh immediately, and taketh away the word that was sown in their hearts." The primary issue here is the place where the seed fell and not the seed itself. The wayside is not the right place for sowing. This is why the birds of the air (or Satan, according to Christ's explanation, came for it immediately). The interesting thing is that, being on the wayside, it would appear that the seed was actually deposited for the birds in the first place, since it was dropped upon the wayside and not on a farmland.

What does this all mean? There are places in which even the best of seeds – words, actions, attitudes – will not germinate, much less grow or produce fruits. We must be aware of this, so we do not dissipate our efforts or blame God, His words, or His ministers, for what has nothing to do with them.

Let me quickly give you an illustration before proceeding to in-depth applications of what we are examining here. Imagine that you were given a powerful bullet to do as you wish. If you threw that bullet at an animal as small as a cat, it would hardly even feel the effect. But take that same bullet, slot into an equally powerful gun and fire it at a huge wild animal – and you would be surprised at the impact it would have. This tells you that what determines the effectiveness of a bullet is often where and how it is used.

You can apply this to seeds and why some refuse to germinate. Most times, the problem is not with the seed but the manner and motive with which it is being sown. I will explain this in detail in the following ways.

THE SPIRITUAL LIFE

Let's begin with our spiritual life. Good works and zealousness for the things of God are essential attributes and indeed requirements of our new life in Christ. Galatians 5:22-23 gives us an outline of manifestations of the Spirit that will be found in the life of everyone who has truly made Jesus the Lord and Savior of His life. Several other passages of the Scripture also emphasize the need for those who have truly been redeemed to demonstrate this by living in newness of life, characterized Christ-like traits. Moreover, we have been assured that the more we sow to the Spirit – consciously making decisions to choose righteousness – the more we will produce fruits towards everlasting life.

Ironically however, there are times that despite all attempts to practice righteousness, the sense of peace and assurance that should naturally characterize anyone living righteously, does not reflect in the lives of some people. They may go to church regularly, pay tithes and offering, volunteer to work for God; yet they lack any sense of relationship with God and continue to experience inner emptiness and dissatisfaction. Despite their best efforts, they still find themselves engaging in sinful habits and addictions that they try so much to hide.

The question is, why can't church attendance, working for God or trying to live a righteous life actually produce peace of mind and a sense of intimacy with God in these people – when these activities are in themselves good seeds? The problem is often that people seek to substitute good works for the real deal, which is genuine salvation in Christ Jesus.

Let me put it in a simple way. No amount of trying to be righteous, being committed to church, donating to the things of God or volunteering for God's work can bring a person into the family of God or make one righteous. These are good seeds, but they will never grow into producing true righteousness. Until a person has a definite, life-changing encounter with Jesus, all their goods works or services to the church or donations to the poor will never produce fruits of righteousness; they will continue to fall by the wayside. This was what Paul lamented about in the early verses of Romans 10, "Brethren, my heart's desire and prayer to God for Israel is, that they might be saved. For I bear them record that they have a zeal of God, but not according to knowledge. For they being ignorant of

God's righteousness, and going about to establish their own righteousness, have not submitted themselves unto the righteousness of God."

So, we have it there; a person must submit himself to the righteousness of God through a conscious acknowledgment of his sinful state and invitation of Christ to be His Savior and Lord before any of His good works can have an impact on his life or count for eternity.

Sometimes people are brought into the church workforce, based on skills, charisma or talents. It so happens that church leaders suddenly get carried away by this zeal and ability that they do not bother to check whether these individuals are born again or not. But soon after, everyone is shocked to discover that despite the seed of commitment to church work that these people have been sowng, as well as the several workers seminars they have been attending, such people have been engaging in immoral, dishonest or criminal activities. And everyone is bewildered. Why should we be shocked that the seeds have been falling by the wayside? The answer is simple: Their singing or preaching or working for God does nothing in their own personal lives because they have not been saved; all their efforts are simply falling by the wayside.

GIVING TO GOD

This is a really crucial area that we must give ample attention. Sometimes people complain that despite their commitment to giving to the things of God, they have not been getting much in return for all their "seed-sowing". They wonder why despite all the promises of bumper harvests that they have received, nothing seems to work as planned. Some of these have been tempted to consider God as a defrauder. But looking at the bulletillustration above, the real problem becomes clear. Giving to God, which is a good seed, is all good and well. But the questions are: where are we doing the giving and with which motive are we doing it?

The simple answer is that many of the financial and material "seeds" that people assume they are sowing into the Kingdom are actually being sown by the wayside. We currently live in an age when supposed men and women of God are seemingly seeking to outdo one another in the "seed-sowing contest". Almost every time one tunes in to a gospel broadcast on radio or TV, what one gets are desperate calls for people to donate to Kingdom work and get a bumper harvest of prosperity in return. Sometimes, scripture passages are twisted to suit the agendas of some of these preachers, who, from all indications, fit into the description in Titus 1:10-11, "For there are many unruly and vain talkers and deceivers…who subvert whole houses, teaching things which they ought not, for filthy lucre's sake."

Sadly, there are people who fall for the gimmicks of these preachers by donating to them or buying some items from them at outrageous rates with the hope of getting some instant miracles. When this does not happen, they think the word of God is probably unreliable, but the truth is that they have merely sown by the wayside.

The Scripture says, in Proverbs 21:16, "The man that wandereth out of the way of understanding shall remain in the congregation of the dead." A "congregation of the dead" is the same as a dead ministry or minister - that is, one that has no real relationship with God or that has lost connection with the Spirit of God. Now, a major characteristic of deadness is lack of growth. Consequently, you cannot be sowing into a ministry that has become more or less a business empire and expect rewards from God. You cannot be donating to a minister whose lifestyle is questionable and who is making a merchandise of God's word and expect God to send any harvest – because such a minister is not working for God but for himself. Sowing into such a ministry reflects lack of understanding and the result is automatic deadness of any "seed" sown. So, friend, be careful of where you sow your seeds, so you can reap the true harvest from the true source of blessings. Not everyone who mentions Christ's name is working for Him!

MOTIVE MATTERS!

But then again, there is the need to consider why people easily find themselves donating to the congregation of the dead. More often than not, it is because of the bogus promises of quick riches and multiplied blessings. This brings us to another key reason why financial and material seeds sown – even into living ministries – sometimes end up by the wayside. This has to do with the motive for giving.

Why exactly do you give to God and His work? Is it out of love for Him and zeal for the progress of His work, or simply because of a hope of immediate blessing? 2 Corinthians 9:6-7, "But this I say, He which soweth sparingly shall reap also sparingly; and he which soweth bountifully shall reap also bountifully. Every man according as he purposeth in his heart, so let him give; not grudgingly, or of necessity: for God loveth a cheerful giver."

God loves a cheerful giver – someone who gives, whether to God or to man, primarily out of love and not out of hope of instant reward. Giving to God is not to be done like playing the lottery; the primary joy should come from the understanding that through our contributions, the church is being strengthened, souls are being saved, members' needs are being met and the ministers of God are being refreshed. But when all we think of when we are giving to God is not what the seed will achieve for the Kingdom, but what it will do for us, then it reflects a lack of a true love for God and His Kingdom. Yet, what the Scripture prescribes as the true way to blessings is, "But seek ye first the kingdom of God, and his righteousness; and all these things shall be added unto you." (Matthew 6:33)

Essentially therefore, when we sow to God's Kingdom, our main concern must be the expansion of the Kingdom and not expansion of our businesses or enlargement of our bank accounts. Yes, all these other expectations and rewards will come but that will only happen if we seek first the Kingdom.

I also know that there are people who may say that God says we should "prove" Him in Malachi 3. But note that the "proving" is not in the giving itself but in the obedience to the command that there is continuous supply of necessities in His house. Malachi 3:10 says, "Bring ye all the tithes into the storehouse, that there may be meat in mine house, and prove me now herewith, saith the Lord of hosts, if I will not open you the windows of heaven, and pour you out a blessing, that there shall not be room enough to receive it."

Do you observe here that God is not presenting himself as the money-doubler that many latter day preachers often project him to be? God never said pay your tithe or sow a seed and I will bless you. He specifically stated the reason the tithe is being brought – that there may be meat in my house. This means that it is this reason that should drive our giving - even of tithes – and not necessarily because we expect multiplied returns.

I know that anyone may ask, "Is it truly possible for anyone to give to God, especially in a sacrificial way, without being concerned about God and His Kingdom?" Yes it is. Paul the Apostle in 1 Corinthians 13:4 says, "And though I bestow all my goods to feed the poor, and though I give my body to be burned, and have not charity, it profiteth me nothing." So, you see it clearly there – if LOVE is not the motive behind any giving – whether to God or to man – then that seed of giving profits nothing, meaning NO GERMINATION.

THE "UNKNOWN" GOD

Paul noted that while looking around the city of Athens, he saw that the people erected an altar and dedicated it to "the Unknown God" (Acts 17:23). In other words, they went the extra mile in erecting that altar, even while acknowledging that it was all a futile gesture. This brings us to the need to reiterate the necessity of prioritizing personal relationship with God above giving to Him. God is not a beggar – and whatever we give to Him is a privilege for us; therefore, it should not be seen as if we are doing Him a favor. This ultimately implies that we cannot give meaningfully and profitably to God on our terms; it has to be on HIS terms.

What do I mean here? God values having the giver of the gift more than the gift. He values our hearts more than our treasures. Paul said something quite instructive about the churches in Macedonia, "For to their power, I bear record, yea, and beyond their power they were willing of themselves; Praying us with much intreaty that we would receive the gift, and take upon us the fellowship of the ministering to the saints. And this they did, not as we hoped, but first gave their own selves to the Lord, and unto us by the will of God." (2 Corinthians 8:3-5).

You see – that's the pattern of giving that God expects of us and the kind giving that yields harvest. There are people who can afford to give anything to God except their lives. They want abundance from God but they do not want to have a personal relationship with God. So they simply keep "sowing" – as often as they are motivated to - while expecting God to "play His part". But God is not a desperate God and such seeds sown hardly get His attention because the manner in which they are sown shows that they are best fitted for the birds of the air and not for the Almighty God. 1 Samuel 15:22 says, "Hath the Lord as great delight in burnt offerings and sacrifices, as in obeying the voice of the Lord? Behold, to obey is better than sacrifice, and to hearken than the fat of rams."

WHEN THE WORD SEEMS TO FAIL

We have, in the previous chapter, dwelt on the power of the seed of the WORD, especially its creative, re-creative and curative power. Here is the truth, however. As the illustration of the bulletreveals, the word functions in relation to the way it is sown. Those whom the word works for are those who have allowed it to work in them. Christ says these signs shall follow them who believe - in my name they shall cast out devils and so on. Note it again: it is those who believe in Him, who have made him their Savior and Lord. Again, when Christ talks of binding and losing or doing wonders with the word, observe that He was specifically addressing the disciples and not the general multitude. So the power of the seed of the word is not meant for everyone. It is meant for the redeemed.

We find a classic demonstration of how the word can

appear not to be effective or in fact, counterproductive in Acts 19:13-16, "Then certain of the vagabond Jews, exorcists, took upon them to call over them which had evil spirits the name of the Lord Jesus, saying, We adjure you by Jesus whom Paul preacheth. And there were seven sons of one Sceva, a Jew, and chief of the priests, which did so. And the evil spirit answered and said, Jesus I know, and Paul I know; but who are ye? And the man in whom the evil spirit was leaped on them, and overcame them, and prevailed against them, so that they fled out of that house naked and wounded."

Here, even the forces of darkness affirm that the word indeed works powerfully against them – on the condition that it is being sown by someone operating from a higher realm in Christ Jesus. But it is not only on demons that the word can work or not work, depending on the sower. Other forces of life answer to this same reality. Positive declarations and affirmations are good, but their effects are neither magical nor automatic. You can make as many affirmations as possible but as long as the earth, the skies and the seas and the forces of nature do not recognize you as one having legitimate authority over them, they may never hearken to you. Indeed, they may instead work against you.

I have seen cases of people who, despite being used to making positive declarations on themselves, still ended their lives in frustration. Therefore, sowing the seed of the word and reaping the expect harvest require developing and nurturing an intimate relationship with the Lord of the word. This way, we can, like Prophet Elijah, confidently declare, "…As the Lord God of Israel liveth, before whom I stand, there shall not be dew nor rain these years, but according to my word" (1 Kings 17:1) – and things will manifest according to our proclamations because we have become one with the Spirit of God within us.

MINISTERIAL, PROFESSIONAL AND ENTREPRENEURIAL SEEDS

Even with the zeal to propagate the gospel and advance God's Kingdom, we must constantly be aware that we are mere workmen or laborers working for a higher authority. It is this authority that we must constantly rely on to prompt, guide and direct our outreaches – otherwise, our efforts will be like the labor of the foolish (Ecclesiastes 10:15).

In Acts 16, we have a very enlightening revelation concerning the missionary efforts of Paul the Apostle: "Now when they had gone throughout Phrygia and the region of Galatia, and were forbidden of the Holy Ghost to preach the word in Asia, After they were come to Mysia, they assayed to go into Bithynia: but the Spirit suffered them not. And they passing by Mysia came down to Troas. And a vision appeared to Paul in the night; There stood a man of Macedonia, and prayed him, saying, Come over into Macedonia, and help us. And after he had seen the vision, immediately we endeavoured to go into Macedonia, assuredly gathering that the Lord had called us for to preach the gospel unto them."

Isn't this interesting? It was Christ who mandated the apostles to go into ALL the world to preach the gospel; and it was the same Christ who specifically gave the assignment of ministering to the Gentiles to Paul the Apostle. Yet, here, we find the Spirit of God FORBIDDING Paul and his companions from sowing the seed of the word in Asia and Bithynia. Rather, through a vision of the night, He directed the missionaries to Macedonia.

The truth is that even though each of these places was a Gentile nation, only Macedonia was ready for the word at that point in time. This means that if Paul and his companions had not been in tune with the Spirit of God and had gone ahead to Asia and Bithynia, whatever seed they would have sown would have most definitely fallen by the "wayside". This, often, is the cause of many frustrating evangelistic outreaches. In as much as we are passionate about reaching the unsaved and planting churches, everything must be done according to the Spirit's leading.

Recently, the media were awash with the tragic story of the young missionary trying to reach an isolated tribe on the North Sentinel Island in the Bay of Bengal. Sadly, he was brutally attacked and killed before he could do anything with the word he had gone there to deliver. From all indications, the tribe – just like Asia and Bithynia – was not ready for the seed of the word. But, of course, its time of ripeness will come and with the help of God's Spirit, we shall receive their cry for help in time.

This same approach to sowing the seed of the gospel is what we must adopt in sowing the seeds of our professional, academic and entrepreneurial investments. Sometimes, the seeds of our efforts in these areas seem to be wasted simply because we choose to depend on our feelings, the opinions of people and the tides of events in the society.

Sometimes we dabble into academic programs, businesses, employments, partnerships and acquisitions that are not meant for us, and then we wonder later why the harvests of satisfaction and all-round fulfillment that we expect are not forthcoming. The challenge is because we tend to forget that we are not ordinary people; we are people of God, governed by the constitution of the heavenly Kingdom. Thus, we cannot be doing things the way everyone else does it. We cannot just jump on any business idea or trending investment opportunity just because everyone is doing it or because it seems "the most natural thing to do."

Here is what you should know. As children of God, we are no longer "natural" beings. We have become supernatural – because he who is born of flesh is flesh, and he who is born of the Spirit is spirit (John 3:6). Consequently, we cannot do things because "that's how it's being done."

Here are two good examples from the Scripture. When a famine broke out in the land of Israel, Naomi and her husband felt that the natural thing to do was to migrate. That was some "seed--sowing" because they expected a harvest – greener pastures. But what did they find? Here's Naomi's testimony, "...Call me not Naomi, call me Mara: for the Almighty hath dealt very bitterly with me. I went out full, and the Lord hath brought me home again empty" (Ruth 1:20-21).

On the positive side, we have this example, "And there was a famine in the land, beside the first famine that was in the days of Abraham. And Isaac went unto Abimelech king of the Philistines unto Gerar. And the Lord appeared unto him, and said, Go not down into Egypt; dwell in the land which I shall tell thee of...Then Isaac sowed in that land, and received in the same year an hundredfold: and the Lord blessed him. And the man waxed great, and went forward, and grew until he became very great" (Genesis 26:1-13).

What Isaac did, sowing in a time of drought, seemed like a very unnatural and irrational thing to do and yet that was what led to immeasurable prosperity for him. When we are in tune with the Spirit of God, circumstances do not have to look right or favorable before we invest. Only God knows the end from the beginning. It is failure to understand this that leads many of us to make investments or exert efforts that the "birds of the air" easily devour, leaving us dejected and disconsolate.

MARRIAGE AND CHILD-RAISING

Taking the step of marriage, as we have seen earlier, is like sowing a seed. The expectation is a harvest of peace, favor and goodly seeds. If this is so, how come that the peace and harmony that many Christian couples crave have perpetually eluded them? The reason is that the seeds of many marital journeys are actually dead on arrival. When a supposed Christian marriage is based on the foundation of lust, quest for riches, or just sympathy – none of which fits into God's purpose for instituting marriage – what germination can one expect? Such a marriage immediately becomes prey to the birds of the air, resulting in experiences that contradict the original purpose of marriage!

The same can be said of raising children. It is common, especially in Christian homes, that children are merely given moral and religious rules to follow, without much emphasis on the necessity of personal salvation and relationship with Christ. Many parents only discover, when it's too late – especially as the children get to teenage years or get to higher institutions - that most of these rules have merely been falling by the wayside. Nothing indeed can substitute for being genuinely born-again. Until we are able to achieve this by continuous teaching, praying and training, there's nothing much that the seeds of mere moral instructions can achieve in the lives of our children.

CALL TO ACTION

Take some time to review the manner and motive with which you have been sowing in all the relevant areas of your life to determine the effectiveness or otherwise. Decide what to jettison, what to imbibe and what to improve upon.

CLOSING THOUGHT

"The labour of the foolish wearieth every one of them, because he knoweth not how to go to the city" (Ecclesiastes 10:15)

The reason the labor of the foolish wearies them is not because they have no passion or zeal but because they lack understanding of how to harness what they have. It is good that we sow seeds but all become wasted if the seeds are sown in a wrong way or at the wrong time. Thus we need the wisdom of God and the guidance of the Holy Spirit to sow right. None of these will be possible without a good relationship with God.

PRAYER POINTS

1. Father, I thank you for the revelation of your word.
2. Lord, guide me with your Spirit to sow aright in all areas of my life.
3. Lord, fill me with wisdom not to sow into the congregation of the dead.
4. Father, fill me with the consciousness of my need of you at all times.
5. Lord, help me not to join the bandwagon of the world but to depend on you in all situations.

4
SEEDS WITH ABORTED GROWTH

"And some fell on stony ground, where it had not much earth; and immediately it sprang up, because it had no depth of earth: But when the sun was up, it was scorched; and because it had no root, it withered away. And some fell among thorns, and the thorns grew up, and choked it, and it yielded no fruit."

Now we are out of the "dead-on-arrival" seed zone. Phew! We have come to the field of seeds that grow. Good news…but wait a minute! How long is this growth we are talking about? A short while. Too bad!

So, why exactly is the growth of seeds in this field being prematurely terminated, leaving no opportunity for maturity and fruit-bearing? Let's quickly do some diagnosis!

TRAGEDY OF CHARISMA WITHOUT CHARACTER

It is a normal law of nature and life in general – a tree that will grow very tall and live many years must have a very deep root; and a building that is designed to be very high must definitely have a very deep and super-solid foundation. When this law is violated, you can be sure that it won't take long before disaster strikes. This is what happens with charisma without character

Take a look again at the case of the seed that fell on stony ground. It springs up quickly but soon dies away because it has no good depth of soil underneath to support the growth. With what can you best compare this analogy in real life situation? Yes, charisma without character!.

"Charisma" comes from the Greek word that means "favor", "gift" or "spiritual grace". It generally refers to a special ability, anointing, gift, talent or any other attractive trait about a person that distinguishes him and draws people to him. Usually, as the name suggests, charisma is a wonderful seed sown into a person's life by God Himself; however, the receiver is expected to develop the requisite character that will support the long-term growth, effectiveness and impacts of this special endowments.

Unfortunately, what happens on many occasions is that "charismatic" people are carried away by the wonders and magnetism of their gifts that they neglect or disregard the training, discipline, humility, wisdom, discretion and godly principles needed to sustain them in the long-run. And the result is usually premature and catastrophic downfall.

Providing insight on this, someone wrote, "Charisma, by its nature, doesn't last long or extend very far. It's like a flash of gunpowder - it produces a quick, blinding light, but then it's gone. The only thing left is smoke. Character, on the other hand, is more like a bonfire. Its effects are long-lasting. It produces warmth and light, and as it continues to burn it gets hotter, giving fuel that burns brighter."

We have many scriptural, historical and contemporary examples of people who, despite being well noted and admired for their giftedness or anointing, ended their careers, callings, ministries and sometimes their lives in scandals, disgrace, defeat and regrets. There are even some whose lack of character only became known after their death and thus had to be posthumously stripped of all honors and glories bestowed on them in their lifetime, leaving them with a permanently ruined memorial. The reason is often because they lack the depth of character needed for enduring success and indelible legacy.

This is why R. C. Samsel wrote, "Character is the foundation stone upon which one must build to win respect. Just as no worthy building can be erected on a weak foundation, so no lasting reputation worthy of respect can be built on a weak character. Without character, all effort to attain dignity is superficial, and results are sure to be disappointing."

Frank Damazio, an author, also wrote: "The Lord cares about a leader's lifestyle and character, not just his gifts and anointing. While the gifts of the Spirit are given freely, character development comes only with time, at great personal effort." While David Abioye of Living Faith Church gave this thought-provoking advice in poetic lines:

Character is the backbone of charisma.

Without character charisma will crash.

Charisma cannot last more than its backing of character.

Charisma is an enduement but character is a virtue to be developed.

You have a duty to develop character that will match your charisma.

Character is the platform that hoist the flag of charisma.

Whatever is endowed can be taken but whatever is developed endures.

The journey of charisma is short but non-assuring but the journey of character is long and enduring.

TAKE AWAY THE THORNS

Christ goes further in His parable to tell us of the seed that falls on the ground full of thorns. Interestingly, despite the fact there is ample time to weed out the thorns, nothing is done, until the seed starts to grow and the thorns choke the growing plants.

Thorns often serve the same purpose as thistles, nettles, tares and little foxes (Songs 2:15) – to frustrate the growth and yield of a beneficial plant. When they are not dealt with early enough, they can turn an otherwise fertile and promising land (life and destiny) into the epicenter of failure and misery. This is why Proverbs 24:30-34 gives this interesting and instructive illustration: "I went by the field of the slothful, and by the vineyard of the man void of understanding; And, lo, it was all grown over with thorns, and nettles had covered the face thereof, and the stone wall thereof was broken down. Then I saw, and considered it well: I looked upon it, and received instruction. Yet a little sleep, a little slumber, a little folding of the hands to sleep: So shall thy poverty come as one that travelleth; and thy want as an armed man."

In exactly the same way the man in the above

illustration was reduced to nothing, that is how many today who have been blessed by God and ought to be excelling in all areas of life are languishing in penury and frustration. But then, we have to admit, as the same illustration shows, that the fault for allowing the thorns to remain rests with the individuals involved.

Thorns manifest in different forms but have the same ultimate purpose – to frustrate whatever good seed that God has deposited in our lives or whatever good work He has begun in our families. How many budding miracles have been thwarted because they were thrown into uncleared grounds! How many prophetic declarations have been aborted at the time they should have manifested because the recipients' lives are littered with unchecked thorns!

FORMS OF THORNS

Thorns could come in form of harmful habits, wrong attitudes, destructive attachments or untreated spiritual issues.

1. Habitual Thorns

Many glorious blessings and destinies have been aborted because of bad habits that were left unchecked. There are people who have missed great opportunities that have been divinely prepared for them because of the habits of laziness, procrastination and lack of punctuality. There are people given to gluttony and have consequently refused to ignore food, when all that's needed to birth their expected testimonies is just a day of fasting. There are people who are so given to sleep that even when the Spirit of God nudges them to pray to birth their miracles or ward off satanic manipulations, they still keep on sleeping till their glories are killed or exchanged (see the case of the two harlots in Solomon's time in 1 Kings 3). There are those who are given to reckless speech, such that they use their tongues to strangle their breakthroughs. There are people who have lost great jobs and relationships because of habits they just won't let go.

2. Attitudinal Thorns

There are people with serious attitudinal problems that sabotage their harvest of blessings. There are people whose unfriendly or intolerant attitude has chased away the destiny-helpers assigned to them. You know, the issue with attitudinal thorns (just like habitual thorns) is that they go with the individual everywhere – and consequently lead to the same results in their lives. That is why you sometimes find people moving from job to job or marriage to marriage, wondering why they can't seem to find joy or rest, and not knowing that what they need to change is not their job or partner but their attitude. This is why someone says, "A bad attitude can literally block love, blessings, and destiny from finding you. Don't be the reason you don't succeed."

Attitudinal thorns can also come in form of a defeatist, pessimistic and cynical approach to life in general and God's word in particular. When a prophetic word is released, whether in a general gathering or one-on-one encounter with a genuine minister of God, and the recipient – for whatever reason – chooses to take it with disbelief, the expected harvest may remain elusive. This was what happened to many of the Israelites, and thus the counsel to us in Hebrews 4:1-2, "Let us therefore fear, lest, a promise being left us of entering into his rest, any of you should seem to come short of it. For unto us was the gospel preached, as well as unto them: but the word preached did not profit them, not being mixed with faith in them that heard it."

3. Destructive Attachments/Environments

The reason some plants never reach maturity is because of the thorns of harmful attachments and environments that many do not want to part with. There are certain individuals, items and environments that exert a negative influence onsome people, preventing them from progressing in their spiritual life or making advancements in their destiny – yet, many do not want to let go. Sometimes, as it was in the case of Abraham, God wants us out of certain environments and relationships so we can reap harvests of blessings, but because we have been so attached, we remain and our blessings are truncated.

There are people who wonder why they are not growing spiritually, despite having been born again for years – yet such people still keep ungodly friends, belong to ungodly associations, watch immoral television shows, listen to corrupting songs, attend functions that defile their minds and so on. There are also those who claim to be waiting on God for miracles but are still consulting horoscopes and other occult mediums – and they wonder why their destiny is being delayed!It is the thorn you have to deal with, friend. See the way the early converts to Christ did it: "And many that believed came, and confessed, and shewed their deeds. Many of them also which used curious arts brought their books together, and burned them before all men: and they counted the price of them, and found it fifty thousand pieces of silver. So mightily grew the word of God and prevailed" (Acts 19:18-20).

Did you see what happened before the word of God could prevail among these people? They had to deal with every potential thorn and threat to their growth and progress. This is the same counsel from God to all who want to see true harvests of blessings, "Sow to yourselves in righteousness, reap in mercy; break up your fallow ground: for it is time to seek the LORD, till he come and rain righteousness upon you" (Hosea 10:12).

Still on environment, it is important that we bring up the issue of child training again. There are times when children indeed become genuinely saved while living with their parents but sadly the parents themselves do not always practice what they preach. Sometimes, they demonstrate traits of hypocrisy and deception; or it could be that the parents are always quarreling, or that they are not careful enough to guide their children on the kind of company they keep or the media exposures they get. The result is often that the children often lose faith and the parents wonder what could have gone wrong. This is why Russell Kolts says, "How we behave toward and around our children has much more influence on their character than if we only tell them about how they should or should not behave."

4. Spiritual Thorns

It also has to be emphasized, though, that there are times when plants of growth, progress and breakthrough are choked to death by thorns that do not necessarily have to do with the individual's choices. Sometimes, it is as a result of defective spiritual foundations, which have been programmed to stifle progress and fruitfulness. Consequently, any seed being dropped into such a life or any effort made by the individual to succeed is truncated before manifestation. I guess you already know the case of Jabez in 1 Chronicles 4:9-10, whose mother had declared sorrow upon his life at birth but ultimately got his breakthrough when he earnestly prayed to God. But I want to show you a more graphic example of how spiritual thorns work.

2 Kings 2:18-22 says, "And when they came again to him, (for he tarried at Jericho,) he said unto them, Did I not say unto you, Go not? And the men of the city said unto Elisha, Behold, I pray thee, the situation of this city is pleasant, as my lord seeth: but the water is naught, and the ground barren. And he said, Bring me a new cruse, and put salt therein. And they brought it to him. And he went forth unto the spring of the waters, and cast the salt in there, and said, Thus saith the Lord, I have healed these waters; there shall not be from thence any more death or barren land. So the waters were healed unto this day, according to the saying of Elisha which he spake."

As the sons of the prophet rightly testified, the land of Jericho was a pleasant place and continuous efforts were being made by the people to plant crops and rear animals, with expectations of abundance. What they got for all their efforts however were unfruitfulness and death. Why? Because a curse had been laid on the land several years before then when the Israelites had overrun the place. It took the intervention of Elisha to undo all the spiritual "thorns" choking the people's efforts and hindering fruitfulness. I pray for you today that every barrier to your harvest be uprooted in Jesus' name!

CALL TO ACTION

Do an assessment of your life and ministry to ascertain areas where you may need more depth of character to back up the gifts of God upon you. Also look out for thorns and "little foxes" that can choke your blessings and map out strategies for uprooting them with God's help.

CLOSING THOUGHT

"Take us the foxes, the little foxes, that spoil the vines: for our vines have tender grapes" (Songs 2:15). It is quite ironical but very instructive that it is the "little foxes" that the writer here is concerned about and not the grown ones. Little foxes have the potential to inflict more harm because they are more likely to be ignored, until they have wreaked untold and sometimes irreparable havoc. This is why you must pay attention to those "little" sins and negative habits that are frequent in your life. They could be the root cause of the delays, disappointments and setbacks that beset your life often.

PRAYER POINTS

1. Almighty Father, help me not to frustrate your grace and gifts upon my life.

2. Empower me, Lord, to develop the strength of character and integrity to sustain your endowments upon me.

3. Help me, Lord, to identify habits and tendencies that can choke my blessings.

4. Strengthen me, Father, to deal with thorns, nettles and little foxes that seek to frustrate my harvest.

5. Uphold me, Father, not to fall from grace to disgrace.

5
PREPARING FOR A BOUNTIFUL HARVEST

"And other fell on good ground, and did yield fruit that sprang up and increased; and brought forth, some thirty, and some sixty, and some an hundred… So is the kingdom of God, as if a man should cast seed into the ground; And should sleep, and rise night and day, and the seed should spring and grow up, he knoweth not how. For the earth bringeth forth fruit of herself; first the blade, then the ear, after that the full corn in the ear. But when the fruit is brought forth, immediately he putteth in the sickle, because the harvest is come."
(Mark 4:8, 26-29)

What a study this has been so far! I am persuaded that our knowledge of how the Kingdom works has expanded. This is the truth of God's word and should be made known, not hoarded. It is to this end that Jesus rebuked the Pharisees and lawyers for taking the key of knowledge from the people, because it is through knowledge that we have access to our inheritance in God. Unfortunately, many are perishing every day due to a lack of knowledge—the knowledge of how this seedtime and harvest principle works.

So far, we have established the indispensability of sowing to reaping. We have comprehensively explored the concept of sowing – such that we now know that it goes far beyond merely donating financial and material resources to churches and preachers. We have equally understood why some seed seem to be wasted and why others grow but never reach maturity or bear fruits. We have a better understanding of the different kinds of "choking thorns" and the need to weed them away to make way for the growing seed to get maximum nourishment.

At this stage, we can safely believe that all that is needed to be done has been done and we are now set to see the fruits of our labors and patience. But I need to point out two things quickly – both of which have been taken from our texts as shown above. First, the yields to be harvested are in different proportions. Second, even in the best of soil (or circumstances) the growth of the seed from germination to fruit-bearing follows a fundamental process.

We have to pay special attention here as we explore

the process of growth and fruit bearing, as well as the factors that determine the rates of yield. Since this is the culmination of our efforts and expectations, we will be taking a very systematic approach, while also using a number of pictorial illustrations to drive home the important messages that abound in this stage. Welcome to your season of harvest!

THE GROWTH PROCESS

Beginning from verse 26 of Mark 4, we are again reminded of the seed concept—the understanding that everything in our life begins with a seed and that we must sow to reap. Now, if that's the case, then we need to know how to manage that process (from seedtime to harvest) the Kingdom way. There are three stages that the passage highlights in verse 28, namely:

1. The blade
2. The ear
3. The full corn

To maximally understand the intricacies of each of these stages, we will consider them biologically and we will liken each of those stages to different organs in our body. This is the route to the revelational insight God led me through as He unveiled this parable and blew up my mind with this grand Kingdom principle.

1. The Blade Stage

Every farmer plants with harvest in view. The purpose of the planting season is to initiate a chain reaction that will culminate in a healthy and bountiful harvest. The first thing that comes up from the planted seed is the blade. We must manage this first stage effectively in order to have, not just a full corn but a very healthy harvest at the end of the day. To do this, as I have mentioned in the introduction, we will journey through basic biological knowledge and make some deductions and applications that will help us to better understand the process involved in this stage. Here's what we know from biology about the blade of a leaf:

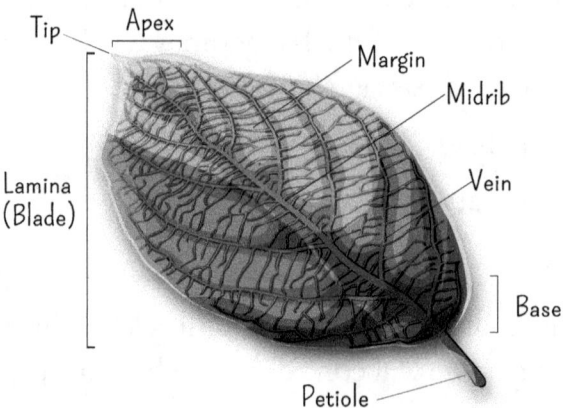

The blade of a leaf is the expanded, thin structure on either side of the midrib. The blade is usually the largest and most conspicuous part of a leaf. The primary function of leaves is to absorb sunLIGHT for the manufacturing of plant sugars in a process called photosynthesis. Leaves develop as a flattened surface in order to present a large area for efficient absorption of LIGHT ENERGY.

The leaf blade is composed of several layers, namely:

a. The Epidermis: This is a layer of thickened tough cells. The primary function of the epidermis is protection of the leaf tissue. Epidermal cells are capable of opening and closing. These cells guard the interior of the leaf and regulate the passage of water, oxygen and carbon dioxide through the leaf. The regulatory cells are called GUARD CELLS. They protect openings in the leaf surface called stoma. The opening and closing of the cells are determined by the WEATHER. Conditions that would cause large water losses from plants (such as high temperature, low humidity, etc) stimulate guard cells to close. Mild weather conditions leave guard cells in an open condition. Guard cells will close in the absence of LIGHT.

Part of the epidermis is the CUTICLE, which is composed of a waxy substance called CUTIN which protects the leaf from dehydration and prevents penetration of some diseases. The amount of cutin is a direct response to sunlight, increasing with increasing light intensity. The waxy cutin also repels water and can shed pesticides if spreader-sticker agents or soap are not used.

b. The Mesophyll: This is the middle layer of the leaf and is located between the upper and lower epidermis. This is the layer in which photosynthesis occurs.

Spiritual Application

You may be wondering, what spiritual applications can we draw out from the above 'biology' lesson about the blade? Good question. Take a look again at the pictures of the leaf blade and ask yourself, "What organ in the human body looks like that?"

THE TONGUE!

As you will see as we unpack this further shortly, it makes absolute spiritual sense to understand the blade stage in this parable in the context of THE HUMAN TONGUE. (Of course, as Jesus Himself said in the preceding parable—the parable of the Sower—the seed is the word. As such, the blade could as well be OUR TONGUE). To further color this parallel with an interesting fact, the human tongue has a blade, too. In fact, anatomically, it is referred to as the tongue blade.

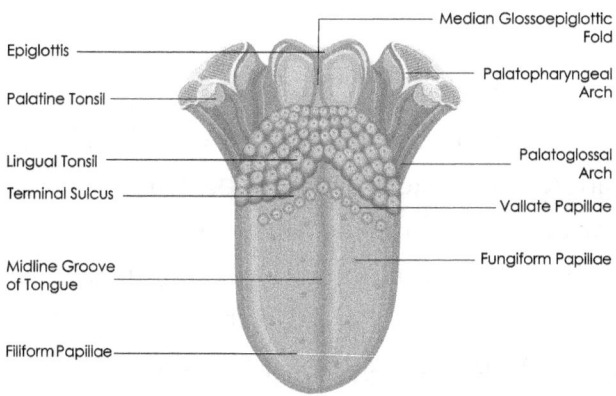

TONGUE

The tongue blade is the part of the top of the tongue right behind the tongue tip (apex). Ladefoged and Maddieson (1996) described it thus: "When the tongue is at rest in a closed mouth, the tongue blade is the part of the tongue that lies directly under the alveolar ridge." This part of the tongue is used in making our speech. (The sounds which are made with the tongue blade are called laminal sounds.)

If we are going to enjoy a bountiful healthy harvest at the FULL CORN STAGE, we need to start by sowing the right seed and engaging our tongue blade adequately. As we continue with this study, some of us will discover our need for a complete speech therapy from the Holy Spirit. May we be willing to yield to His dealings!

2. The Tongue Blade

Now, let's explore the tongue blade further. We already considered the blade stage biologically by identifying the primary function of the leaf blade—to collect sunlight and water so that the plant can develop very well. The sunlight and water which a leaf blade receives and preserves for a plant to grow is symbolic of God's word. The scripture tells us that the word of the Lord is a lamp, a light, and also water to us. Following the thread of spiritual deductions from the biological symbolisms of the leaf blade cum tongue blade, we discover that the way we also bring light and water to our seedlings is by using our tongue positively.

We previously discuss the power of our words as seeds. Now, we'll go further to examine the roles our words play in the growth and fruitfulness of our seeds. The scriptures tell us:

"He that keepeth his mouth keepeth his life: but he that openeth wide his lips shall have destruction." (Proverbs 13:3)

"Death and life are in the power of the tongue: and they that love it shall eat the fruit thereof." (Proverbs 18:21)

"For he that will love life, and see good days, let him refrain his tongue from evil, and his lips that they speak no guile:" (1 Peter 3:10)

See how powerful our tongue is? With our tongue, we can shape our lives and challenge every negative tongue speaking negativity into our lives. We can do this by either of two ways:

1. Keeping our matters to ourselves; and

2. Vehemently opposing every word that is contrary to what we are believing God for.

Isaiah 54:17 says, "No weapon that is formed against thee shall prosper; and every tongue that shall rise against thee in judgment thou shalt condemn. This is the heritage of the servants of the Lord, and their righteousness is of me, saith the Lord."

As earlier mentioned, the key function of the leaf blade has to do with its retention of light and water. What would this look like in our practical experience?

THE SOURCE OF LIGHT

1. Salvation.

Salvation is our number one source of light. The Scripture tells us what happened at the moment of Paul's conversion, "And as he journeyed, he came near

Damascus: and suddenly there shined round about him a light from heaven:" (Acts 9:3)

Earlier on, John says about Jesus, "In him was life; and the life was the light of men." (John 1:4)

This means that making Christ one's Lord and Saviour signals the end of darkness and the works of darkness in the person's life. Christ Himself says it unequivocally, "I am the light of the world: he that followeth me shall not walk in darkness, but shall have the light of life" (John 8:12).

2. The Word of the Spirit.

The word of God illumines our heart and the world around us, making us to have a better perspective of our experiences and encounters. Hence, the Psalmist says, "Thy word is a lamp unto my feet, and a light unto my path." (Psalms 119:105)

He further says, "The entrance of thy words giveth light; it giveth understanding unto the simple" (Psalms 119:130).

THE SOURCE OF WATER

A thriving relationship with the Lord ensures that our lives are continually watered, so that we know no dryness, famine or withering.

Psalm 1:1-3 says, "Blessed is the man that walketh not in the counsel of the ungodly, nor standeth in the way of sinners, nor sitteth in the seat of the scornful. But his delight is in the law of the Lord; and in his law doth he meditate day and night. And he shall be like a tree planted by the rivers of water, that bringeth forth his fruit in his season; his leaf also shall not wither; and whatsoever he doeth shall prosper."

Isaiah 12:3 promises, "Therefore with joy shall ye draw water out of the wells of salvation."

Ephesians 5:26 also mentions the process of our sanctification and cleansing by water, "That he might sanctify and cleanse it with the washing of water by the word,"

3. The Ear Stage

"For the earth bringeth forth fruit of herself; first the blade, then the ear, after that the full corn in the ear" (Mark 4:28).

To understand this stage, we will journey through a basic biological knowledge of a plant's ear and thereafter proceed to make some deductions and applications. Here's what we know from biology about the ear of a plant:

Seedtime and Harvest

An ear is the grain-bearing tip part of the stem of a cereal plant, such as wheat or maize. It can also refer to "a prominent lobe in some leaves".

The ear is a spike, consisting of a central stem on which grows tightly packed rows of flowers. These develop into fruits containing the edible seeds. In corn, it is protected by leaves called husks.

In some species (including wheat), unripe ears contribute significantly to photosynthesis, in addition to the leaves lower down the plant.

A parasite known as Anguina tritici (ear cockle) specifically affects the ears on wheat and rye by destroying the tissues and stems during growth.

The primary function of the ear is to act as the carrier or the space in which the fruit develops into a harvest. The ear produces the connection between the outside world to what goes on in the inside. For this reason it must be protected from any parasitical attack because parasites are known to attack this stage to hinder the ear from functioning the way it should.

Spiritual Application

As we did with the blade stage, we want to identify the human body organ which corresponds to this 'ear process' in us as believers.

The answer to that couldn't be more obvious: The human ear! The ear stage has everything to do with the two ears on either sides of our head.

THE HUMAN EAR

Again, to further understand this correlation, we will consider a bit of the anatomy of the human ear. The first thing for us to understand is that the primary function of the ear is for hearing and balance—the latter being one of the functions performed by the ear of any plant—and they both have apexes, too.

The human ear is an advanced and very sensitive organ in the human body. Its function is to transmit and transduce sound to the brain through its different parts: the outer ear, the middle ear, and the inner ear. The major task of the ear is to detect, transmit and transduce sound. Another very important function of the ear is to maintain our sense of balance. This part of our body is so significant spiritually and shares a commonality with the Old Testament tabernacle by virtue of also being divided into three compartments: the outer ear (outer court), the middle ear (inner court) and the inner ear (Holy of Holies).

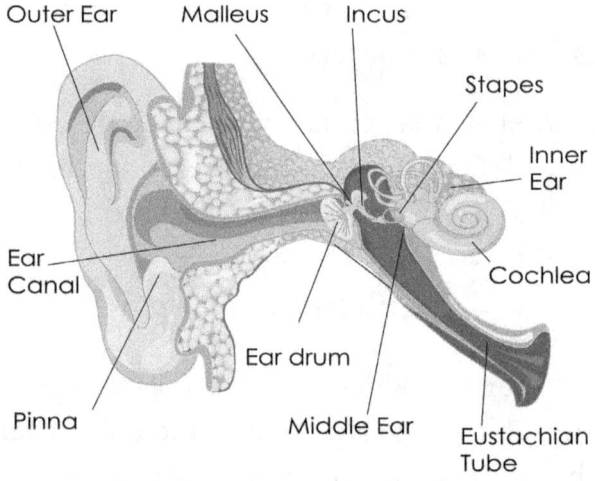

The outer ear /outer court

This is referred to as the pinna. The pinna is the only visible part of the ear (the auricle) with its special helical shape. It is the first part of the ear that interacts with sound. The function of the pinna is to act as a kind of funnel which assists in directing the sound further into the ear. Likewise, the outer court was a type of a holding area. Unfortunately, not very many people make it past that phase.

The middle ear /inner court

The primary function of the middle ear is to efficiently transfer acoustic energy from compression waves in air to fluid–membrane waves within the cochlea. It is a deeper process compared to what happens at the outer ear. In the same vein, the inner court was on a higher level than the outer court. It was more difficult to proceed to the inner court; all the necessary requirements must be met, first.

The inner ear /Holy of Holies

The inner ear (internal ear, auris interna) is the innermost part of the vertebrate ear. In vertebrates, the inner ear is mainly responsible for sound detection and balance. In mammals, it consists of the bony labyrinth, a hollow cavity in the temporal bone of the skull with a system of passages comprising two main functional parts:

1. The cochlea — this is dedicated to hearing; converting sound pressure patterns from the outer ear into electrochemical impulses which are passed on to the brain via the auditory nerve.

2. The vestibular system — this is dedicated to balance.

The 'Holy of Holies' in the Hebrew Bible refers to the inner sanctuary of the Tabernacle where God dwelt. The Ark of Covenant is said to have contained the Ten Commandments, manna, and Aaron's rod that budded — all significant and symbolic. The inner ear, like the 'Holy of Holies', is where everything that affects our harvest happens. It is up to us what we allow up there.

The reason for all these anatomical details is basically to let us know how much God wants us to protect and prevent junks from entering our ears. I said all these to show us why our hearing is very important to this stage of development. All the faith you will ever need for a bountiful harvest comes from your hearing, and what you hear will affect your balance (your spiritual stability).

"So then faith cometh by hearing, and hearing by the word of God. But I say, Have they not heard? Yes verily, their sound went into all the earth, and their words unto the ends of the world" (Romans 10:17-18).

Mind Your Hearing

Job made a statement that underscores the link between our hearing and our ability to see the manifestation of our harvest. He said to the Lord, "I have heard of thee by the hearing of the ear: but now mine eye seeth thee" (Job 42:5). While he's making the point that what we see supersedes what we hear, he is also implying that what we eventually get to see (our harvest) is absolutely linked to what we've been hearing. In fact, we could gather from that verse that until our ears can hear, our eyes may never see our full harvest.

We see a good example of this in Samuel; God did not reveal His future plans to him until his hearing was improved and attuned to understand what the Spirit was telling him.

1 Samuel 3:7-10 says, "Now Samuel did not yet know the Lord, neither was the word of the Lord yet revealed unto him. And the Lord called Samuel again the third time. And he arose and went to Eli, and said, Here am I; for thou didst call me. And Eli perceived that the Lord had called the child. Therefore Eli said unto Samuel, Go, lie down: and it shall be, if he call thee, that thou shalt say, Speak, Lord; for thy servant heareth. So Samuel went and lay down in his place. And the Lord came, and stood, and called as at other times, Samuel, Samuel. Then Samuel answered, Speak; for thy servant heareth."

Until your hearing improves, you are not in a position to get the kind of instructions that will bring you closer to your harvest.

Let's consider the EAR STAGE a little further by asking ourselves this important question: How can my ears detect and reject bad information immediately?

We find this possibility in the book of Job. Job 34:3 highlights this vital ability of our ears—the ability to 'taste' words, just in a similar fashion to how we use our tongue to taste food. When you taste something with your tongue and find it unpalatable, do you keep on chewing? No. You automatically spit it out! In like manner, you can develop your ears to taste words and reject that which is unwholesome as soon as you hear it.

"For the ear trieth words, as the mouth tasteth meat" (Job 34:3).

The Amplified Bible puts it this way, "For the ear puts words to the test As the palate tastes food."

YOUR HEARING DETERMINES YOUR HARVEST

Let us consider some benefits that we stand to gain when our hearing is healthy and in tune with God's voice.

1. You can easily determine the appropriate timing of your seed.

"Who among you will give ear to this? who will hearken and hear for the time to come?" (Isaiah 42:23).

2. You will gain unusual wisdom which will improve your harvest.

"So that thou incline thine ear unto wisdom, and apply thine heart to understanding" (Proverbs 2:2)

3. You will be well versed in the knowledge of how the Kingdom of God works.

"The heart of the prudent getteth knowledge; and the ear of the wise seeketh knowledge." (Proverbs 18:15)

4. You will heed reproof (correction) and improve your harvest.

"The ear that heareth the reproof of life abideth among the wise. He that refuseth instruction despiseth his own soul: but he that heareth reproof getteth understanding." (Proverbs 15:31-32)

"The Lord God hath opened mine ear, and I was not rebellious, neither turned away back." (Isaiah 50:5)

5. You will know your covenant rights and your standing with God.

"Incline your ear, and come unto me: hear, and your soul shall live; and I will make an everlasting covenant with you, even the sure mercies of David." (Isaiah 55:3)

6. You will have a sense of direction and not labor in vain.

"And thine ears shall hear a word behind thee, saying, This is the way, walk ye in it, when ye turn to the right hand, and when ye turn to the left." (Isaiah 30:21)

7. Your hearing will help you to stop all poisonous information at the door.

"For the ear trieth words, as the mouth tasteth meat" (Job 34:3).

CLOSING THOUGHT

"Let your speech be always with grace, seasoned with salt, that ye may know how ye ought to answer every man." (Colossians 4:6)

Let the words you speak be ALWAYS—not sometimes, not once in a while—always with GRACE, and SEASONED WITH SALT. Why is this important? It is important because the health, quality and longevity of the blade that will emanate from your seed depends on how you use your tongue blade. Speak right.

CALL TO ACTION

Take a complete inventory of your life and evaluate the result of the good and bad use of your tongue.

Also, try to identify two or three parasites that can mess up your harvest at the ear stage.

PRAYER POINTS

1. Father, help me so that my speech will be always with grace and seasoned with salt.

2. Father, give me the grace to be able to bridle my tongue at all times

3. Father, awaken my spiritual sensitivity to be able to know per time, what the Spirit is saying.

4. Lord, restore unto me the balance and stability that the enemy has robbed me of in Jesus' name.

5. Father let my path shine brighter until that perfect day.

6

YOUR HEART AND YOUR HARVEST

"And these are they which are sown on good ground; such as hear the word, and receive it, and bring forth fruit, some thirtyfold, some sixty, and some an hundred." (Mark 4:20)

What an adventure we have been through studying this wonderful topic. This understanding of how the Kingdom works has improved my understanding about every aspect of my life, and I hope you share the same experience. God is a consistent God. He gives everyone equal opportunities to excel - hence this principle of seed time and harvest time. The clergy are not supposed to be operating on one level and the laity on another; the principle levels the playing field for all.

Jesus told us that no matter what we sow, there are three stages of development: first the BLADE stage, second the EAR stage, and third the FULL CORN stage. We have successfully looked at the first two stages with a keen understanding of what happens at those stages and how we can influence the outcomes of our harvest from those stages. In this chapter, we will begin to look at THE FULL CORN STAGE, and specifically how the state of our heart affects our harvest.

We have highlighted the importance of understanding what happens at each stage and also learned which part of our body needs to be engaged at each stage in order to maximize our harvest. For the blade stage, our tongue was the organ of focus; for the ear stage, it was our ears; and for this full corn stage, which organ in our body do you reckon needs to be engaged? Our HEART! (Sometimes referred to as our MIND).

Just as we considered the tongue and the ear physiologically in order to understand their spiritual significance in their respective processes, we will do the same with the heart. Our physiological understanding of the heart and how it functions will be the foundation of our knowledge of our SPIRITUAL HEART being the 'good ground' at any given time. We will thus proceed to learn something about our heart structure and function and how that relates to us maximizing the FULL CORN STAGE.

WHAT THE BIBLE SAYS ABOUT OUR HEART

Proverbs 4:23 counsels, "Keep thy heart with all diligence; for out of it are the issues of life".

There are three gates through which our heart receives information: THE MOUTH GATE (corresponding to the TONGUE BLADE in the blade stage), THE EAR GATE (corresponding to our EAR in the ear stage) and the EYE GATE which we will talk much about later. In Proverbs 4:23 quoted above, the wisest man that ever lived in his generation (Solomon), is encouraging us to keep our heart "with all diligence". Why? Because out of it flows the issues of life! Every harvest you will ever get is tied to the condition of your heart.

THE FULL CORN STAGE

Let us briefly familiarize ourselves with the anatomy of the heart. The primary function of the heart is to carry oxygen and distribute blood to the vital organs of our body for nourishment. This is, in fact, is the same function performed by the ground to any plant—carrying oxygen for aeration and nutrients to the plant.

Heart Definition

The heart is a muscular organ that pumps blood throughout the body. It is located in the middle cavity of the chest, between the lungs. In most people, the heart is located on the left side of the chest, beneath the breastbone. The heart is composed of smooth muscles. It has four chambers which contract in a specific order, allowing the human heart to pump blood from the body to the lungs and back again with high efficiency. The heart also contains "pacemaker" cells which fire nerve impulses at regular intervals, prompting the heart muscle to contract.

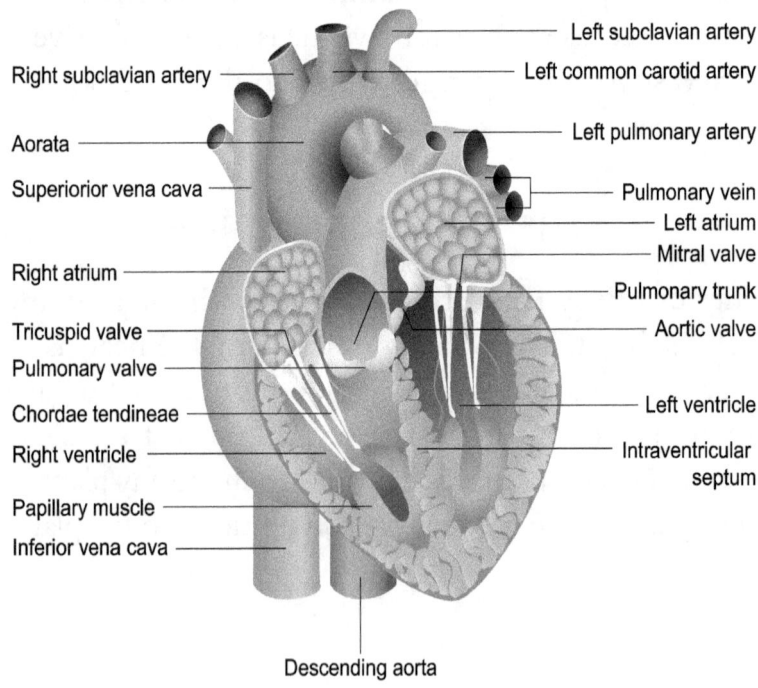

The heart is one of the most vital and delicate organs in the body. If it does not function properly, all other organs – including the brain – begin to die from lack of oxygen within just a few minutes. As of 2009, the most common cause of death in the world was heart disease, which often occurs as a result of age or lifestyle.

Function of the Heart

The heart pumps blood through our immense and complicated circulatory systems at high pressure. It is a truly impressive feat of engineering, as it must circulate about five liters of blood through a 1,000 miles worth of blood vessels each minute! The pumping action of the heart allows the movement of many substances between organs in the body, including nutrients, waste products, hormones and other chemical messengers. However, arguably the most important substance it circulates is oxygen.

The Correlation

1. The heart pumps blood to all our vital organs; similarly, plants receive all their nutrients from the ground.

2. The heart needs oxygen to be active and productive; similarly, the ground provides the necessary oxygen needed to aerate the plant.

3. The most common cause of death in the world is heart disease; similarly, the most common 'harvest killer' is heart disease (the condition of our heart).

4. Most cases of heart disease occur as a result of lifestyle; likewise, the most common heart disease in the Kingdom is usually tied to our lifestyles. (We will explore this later as there are four categories involved).

I say all these to come to this very important point with regards to enjoying a full harvest: we need the FRESH BREATH from the Holy Ghost, and the BLOOD OF JESUS to make our hearts GOOD GROUNDS and to fend off any parasitic infestation while providing us with the communion that brings vitality to our harvest.

How do we get these vital "heart-sanitizers"? We must make conscious efforts to wait upon the Lord in prayer and meditating on His word. When our hearts are thus purified, it paves the way for the ultimate catalyst of a bumper harvest, which we are considering next.

FAITH: THE PARAMOUNT DETERMINANT OF HARVEST

Mark 4:27 says, "And should sleep, and rise night and day, and the seed should spring and grow up, he knoweth not how."

While the above verse in our passage of focus alludes to the fact that the process that leads to our harvest is a function of God's sovereignty and providence, it does not negate the fact that God has given us the opportunity to, through the knowledge of the truth, access all that Jesus died for. Reaching our full potential and getting maximum harvests depends on how well we are able to guard our tongue, our ear and our heart. Ultimately however, our harvest is determined by how well our heart cooperates with God in faith. God wants us to fully yield our heart to the divine seed (which is His word) knowing full well that He upholds all things—not some things—by the word of His power.

Let's recall that Jesus specifically pointed out that the harvest potential is in levels—30, 60 and 100-fold. The question then is, how do we enjoy a hundred-fold return? We have the answer in Hebrews 11:1-3, 6, "Now faith is the substance of things hoped for, the evidence of things not seen. For by it the elders obtained a good report. Through faith we understand that the worlds were framed by the word of God, so that things which are seen were not made of things which do appear...But without faith it is impossible to please him: for 1`he that cometh to God must believe that he is, and that he is a rewarder of them that diligently seek him."

Hebrews 11, considered to be the hall of fame of faith narrates how faith generals in the scriptures used their heart to believe God and by so doing were able to accomplish extraordinary feats. The chapter begins by telling us what faith is and in the second verse, reveals to us how our forefathers in the faith obtained a good report. "By faith," the chapter continues, "the worlds were framed by the word of God." By the time we get to verse 6, we learn that "Without faith, it is impossible to please God". It can be inferred therefore that without a good ground, which is our heart, it is impossible to please God.

However, even in good grounds, productivity level varies as Jesus points out with His analogy of a 30-, 60-, and 100-fold harvest. I believe that this difference in productivity levels has something to do with our measure of faith. Paul says in his epistle to the Romans, "God has apportioned to each a degree of faith" (Romans 12:3 AMP). By implication, therefore, it is to the extent that we develop the degree of faith that has been apportioned to us that our level of harvest is determined.

Here is what the passage in Romans says in full: "For by the grace [of God] given to me I say to everyone of you not to think more highly of himself [and of his importance and ability] than he ought to think; but to think so as to have sound judgment, as God has apportioned to each a degree of faith [and a purpose designed for service]" (Romans 12:3 AMP).

As earlier mentioned, it is the extent to which we develop the degree of faith that has been apportioned to us that determines our level of harvest. There are four sub-categories in this regard:

1. No faith

2. Little faith

3. Great faith

4. The spirit of faith

We will consider them one after the other.

1. No Faith

In Mark 9:19, Jesus lamented the lack of faith of His disciples: "He answereth him, and saith, O faithless generation, how long shall I be with you? how long shall I suffer you? bring him unto me" (Mark 9:19).

Here, Christ referred to the disciples as being faithless. The story further underscores the fact that without faith, it is impossible to please God. In fact, without faith, it is impossible to see any harvest in your life. A life of doubt is a very risky and absolutely unproductive lifestyle; it's not meant for us.

2. Little Faith

In another scenario, Jesus was sleeping in the inner part of the ship (see Matthew 8), and left His disciples in charge of affairs while He rested in preparation for the next outreach. Before long, He was being awakened by His disciples because of a wind. In rebuking them this time around, He told them that they were of a little faith. (Perhaps, they experienced a faith surge from nothing to little when they saw Peter's mother-in-law healed.) However, "little faith" will result in a "little harvest"—say 30%—at the end of the day.

"And he saith unto them, Why are ye fearful, O ye of little faith? Then he arose, and rebuked the winds and the sea; and there was a great calm." (Matthew 8:26)

Who has this type of heart?

1. A young convert
2. A believer who is not conversant with the Word
3. A good believer who operates under the spirit of fear.
4. All of us at the moment of our weakness.

3. Great Faith

The Bible tells us of a woman who was desperate for a miracle and went to see Jesus for a divine intervention. The most striking detail we have from the scripture about this woman is that she's not even in a covenant relationship with Jesus (by virtue of her ethnicity), but when she persisted, Jesus observed her faith and described it as great.

"But he answered and said, I am not sent but unto the lost sheep of the house of Israel. Then Jesus answered and said unto her, O woman, great is thy faith: be it unto thee even as thou wilt. And her daughter was made whole from that very hour" (Matthew 15:24, 28).

The woman secured her daughter's healing, in spite of the fact that she was outside a covenant relationship. I believe it is safe to conclude that her 'great faith' produced what Jesus referred to as a 60-fold increase.

Applying that to us as present-day believers, it is quite unfortunate that many of us pray and believe God for a miracle but choose to keep operating outside our covenant rights. For example, the Scriptures tell us to bring all the tithes into the house of God—which is an expression of our covenant responsibilities in our covenant relationship with God. Many believers are explaining that principle away now, choosing instead to excuse themselves from consistent sacrificial giving in God's house. No wonder they are limited to a 60-fold return category. Our covenant relationship could afford us much more!

4. The Spirit of Faith

This is the faith level that guarantees a 100-fold return. Going back to the point made ealier, Jesus has promised to give us a mouth and a wisdom that cannot be gainsaid or resisted by any satanic influence. That is how the Spirit of faith operates! This faith is a function of how well we use our tongue, our ear and our heart altogether. Paul taught us about this Spirit of faith, pointing out that when we have it, we will begin to speak what we believe and not what we see. Our sight becomes irrelevant when we begin to operate in the full measure of the spirit of faith.

"We having the same spirit of faith, according as it is written, I believed, and therefore have I spoken; we also believe, and therefore speak" (2 Corinthians 4:13).

Who has this kind of heart?

1. A believer who's using his or her tongue judiciously.
2. A believer who's filled with boldness to dare the status quo.

CALL TO ACTION

Go through Hebrews 11 again and make a list of all the things that were accomplished by faith as recorded in the chapter.

Note also that it is very important to maintain a good heart at every stage in our Christian walk; therefore, be mindful of your ground and guard against spiritual slumber.

While men slept, the enemy _____. (Search the scripture and fill in the blank)

CLOSING THOUGHT

"Who through faith subdued kingdoms, wrought righteousness, obtained promises, stopped the mouths of lions, Quenched the violence of fire, escaped the edge of the sword, out of weakness were made strong, waxed valiant in fight, turned to flight the armies of the aliens." (Hebrews 11:33-34)

Take a look at what the Spirit of faith can do on the good ground of our heart once we put our tongue, ear and heart to a very good use. Start engaging the spirit of faith in your daily life. Shalom.

Seedtime and Harvest

PRAYER POINTS

1. Father, help my heart to be right with you, so that I can have a good ground that guarantees a bountiful harvest.

2. Father, help me to manage all the gates that lead to my heart in Jesus name.

3. Father, please take me to the ground that is higher than I in faith.

4. Father, help me to bridle my tongue, so that I can only say what you say.

5. Father, help me to stay awake spiritually in this end time.

7

SURE WAYS TO BUILD UP YOUR FAITH

"Then said I, Lo, I come: in the volume of the book it is written of me" (Psalms 40:7)

As we have noted repeatedly in the preceding chapters of this book, the principles in the Kingdom of God are based on the one principle of seedtime and harvest. In Psalm 40:7, the psalmist reveals to us that there's a 'volume of the book' that has been written about us, and the way we discover and actualize what has been written concerning us is also by engaging this seedtime and harvest principle.

As Jesus explained, there are three stages of development from seeding to harvesting and we will see how these stages come together in discovering and fulfilling that which has been written concerning us in the 'volume of the book'. The first stage is the

BLADE STAGE, which, as we have established, relates to our tongue at work. This is how we decode what is written concerning us in the 'volume of the book'.

Again, the psalmist says "My heart is inditing a good matter...my tongue is the pen of a ready writer." (Psalm 45:1) It's instructive that he equates our tongue with the pen of a ready writer. In other words, we write our destinies with our tongue!

The second stage is the EAR STAGE which has to do with our ear. For your heart to indite (compose) a good matter, your hearing must be in tune with heaven.

Finally, is the FULL CORN STAGE, which has to do with the nature of our heart. Our hearts must be cultivated to be a good ground—a place where 'good matters' can be indited, by the virtue of what our tongue is writing and what our ear is hearing.

Jesus infers in our passage of reference (Mark 4:27-28) that the knowledge and understanding of the seedtime and harvest principle should lead us to a place of rest and assurance whereby we can sleep soundly with the assurance that our harvest is guaranteed.

In the preceding chapters on the FULL CORN STAGE, we have identified and considered the four stages of faith that determine our degrees of harvest. We identified the 'no faith', 'little faith', 'great faith' and the 'spirit of faith' categories. With faith being so foundational to our fruitfulness and harvest, Jude's admonition in Jude 20 comes alive anew: "But ye, beloved, building up yourselves on your most holy faith, praying in the Holy Ghost," (Jude 1:20).

The question we are answering in this chapter, therefore, is simply this: How do I build up my faith in God? Follow me and let's explore together.

SEVEN WAYS TO BUILD UP YOUR FAITH

1. Be born again.

Without God, we belong to the 'no faith' category; when we become born again, Christ dwells in our heart by faith, and that is how we get the measure of faith.

"That Christ may dwell in your hearts by faith; that ye, being rooted and grounded in love," (Ephesians 3:17.**2. Study the word.**

Faith comes by hearing and hearing the word of God. "In the beginning was the Word, the Word was with God and the Word was God" (John 1:1). When you study the word, you are simply studying God. So, study until you are approved!

"Study to shew thyself approved unto God, a workman

that needeth not to be ashamed, rightly dividing the word of truth" (2 Timothy 2:15).

3. Love God and people.

Faith works by love. When you love, the power of faith is unleashed in your life. Love drives faith to its maximum yield point as it delivers in our lives.

"For in Jesus Christ neither circumcision availeth any thing, nor uncircumcision; but faith which worketh by love." (Galatians 5:6)

4. Have absolute trust in God.

The Scripture says, "God cannot lie." God even swore by two immutable things by which it is impossible for Him to lie. You can trust Him.

"That by two immutable things, in which it was impossible for God to lie, we might have a strong consolation, who have fled for refuge to lay hold upon the hope set before us:" (Hebrews 6:18)

5. Meditate on the word.

The word of the Lord must not depart from our heart and mouth; we are to meditate on it day and night to have good success, which is the result of the Spirit of faith. Psalms 1:1-3 paints a great picture of what this looks like: "Blessed is the man that walketh not in the counsel of the ungodly, nor standeth in the way of sinners, nor sitteth in the seat of the scornful. But his delight is in the law of the Lord; and in his law doth he meditate day and night. And he shall be like a tree planted by the rivers of water, that bringeth forth his fruit in his season; his leaf also shall not wither; and whatsoever he doeth shall prosper."

6. Pray always in the Holy Spirit.

We are instructed to build our faith by praying in the Holy Spirit.

"But ye, beloved, building up yourselves on your most holy faith, praying in the Holy Ghost" (Jude 1:20).

7. Learn to forgive and let go.

Job forgave his friends and faith for recovery surged in his heart. Believe God for Job's order of revival—absolute and double restoration – as you forgive offences and let go of every root of bitterness.

"And the Lord turned the captivity of Job, when he prayed for his friends: also the Lord gave Job twice as much as he had before."(Job 42:10)

CALL TO ACTION

Where do you stand? How strong or shaky is your faith? Put to practice the counsel of Haggai 1:5 by taking some quiet time to honestly consider your ways.

CLOSING THOUGHT

"Now therefore thus saith the Lord of hosts; Consider your ways." (Haggai 1:5)

The Lord is near. Let us seek first the Kingdom of God and its righteousness, and, as Jesus assured, all other things shall be added to us. Shalom.

PRAYER POINTS

1. Father, help my faith to grow and help me starve my unbelief to death in the name of Jesus.

2. Father, open my eyes to behold the wonderful things in Your Word that will build my faith.

3. Lord, purge my heart of all killers of faith, Jesus' name.

4. Lord, quicken me from within with the Spirit of faith.

5. Father, make me a champion of faith in Jesus' name.

8
OPEN THE EYES OF MY HEART

> *"The eyes of your understanding being enlightened; that ye may know what is the hope of his calling, and what the riches of the glory of his inheritance in the saints."* (Ephesians 1:18)

What an eye opener this study has been as we journey into a better understanding of what "seedtime and harvest" really means. However, what does it a farmer who, having done all that is required in the seedtime, is blinded from recognizing his harvest when it comes? We need to be able to see what God is doing when our harvest has fully come. The Psalmist tells us that God is the only One that can open our eyes so that we can behold wondrous things hidden to our physical eyes. We shall see how this happens shortly.

In the meantime, let's do a quick recap of what we have learned so far concerning our season of harvest. The BLADE STAGE is where it all begins—it is the first true evidence that our harvest is on the way; it corresponds with the use of our tongue. The scripture tells us that we should open our mouth wide so that our lives could be filled with good things.

"I am the Lord thy God, which brought thee out of the land of Egypt: open thy mouth wide, and I will fill it." (Psalms 81:10)

The EAR STAGE follows that. This stage has to do with how we hear so that we can get understanding, in accordance with Solomon's counsel: "Wisdom is the principal thing; therefore get wisdom: and with all thy getting get understanding." (Proverbs 4:7)

Finally is the FULL CORN STAGE. This stage is a matter of the HEART. Our heart is supposed to be the 'good ground' needed for our harvest to mature. The scripture reveals to us that the way to make our harvest steady and maximal (producing at 100% potential) is for our heart to pant after God as a deer pants after the water brooks.

"As the hart panteth after the water brooks, so panteth my soul after thee, O God." (Psalms 42:1)

RECOGNIZING YOUR HARVEST

Here, we shall be looking at how to see with our inner eyes when our harvest is ready. We read of an instance when the disciples of Jesus were not able to see the very ripe harvest that was right before them. Jesus had to call their attention to it. Let us look at the scripture together.

"Say not ye, There are yet four months, and then cometh harvest? behold, I say unto you, Lift up your eyes, and look on the fields; for they are white already to harvest." (John 4:35)

Clearly, from that text, the disciples were deferring the harvest season to the future—four more months! Why? They could not see that the harvest was right there already! This surely has some spiritual connotation and application with our subject of discussion in this book. It highlights the necessity for us to "lift up our spiritual eyes" to see what our field looks like. This ability to recognize our harvest is very important, otherwise we will continue to pray for what is right at our doorstep.

Michael W. Smith composed a beautiful song titled "Open the Eyes of My Heart"—that should be our heart cry! The eyes of our heart must be opened for us to see the harvest on our good ground. Jesus died on the cross so that the veil covering the Holy of Holies might be torn so that we can have an unlimited access to behold our rich inheritance in Him.

So, in consonance with the approach we have employed in unpacking the three stages of the seedtime and harvest process—likening each stage to the functioning of an organ in our human body—we will do a little study on the anatomy of our physical eyes, so that we can gain insight as to what we need for our spiritual eyes to be opened.

Anatomy of The Eye

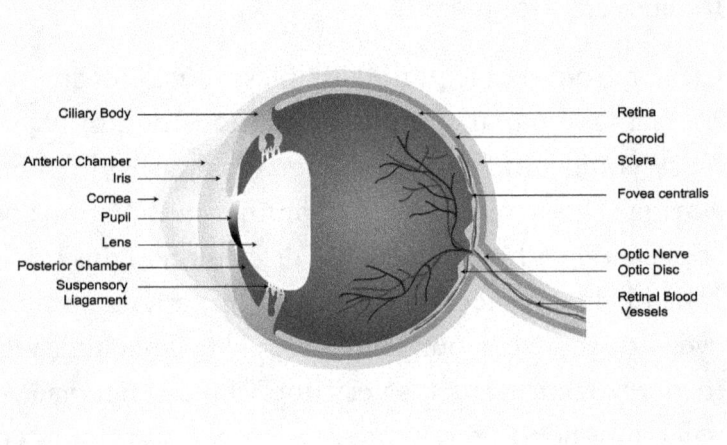

The eye is our organ of sight. The eye has a number of components which includes but are not limited to the cornea, iris, pupil, lens, retina, macula, optic nerve, choroid and vitreous.

1. Cornea: clear front window of the eye that transmits and focuses light into the eye.

2. Iris: colored part of the eye that helps regulate the amount of light that enters.

3. Pupil: dark aperture in the iris that determines how much light is let into the eye.

4. Lens: transparent structure inside the eye that focuses light rays onto the retina.

5. Retina: nerve layer that lines the back of the eye, senses light, and creates electrical impulses that travel through the optic nerve to the brain.

6. Macula: small central area in the retina that contains special light-sensitive cells and allows us to see fine details clearly.

7. Optic nerve: connects the eye to the brain and carries the electrical impulses formed by the retina to the visual cortex of the brain.

8. Vitreous: clear, jelly-like substance that fills the middle of the eye.

From the details above, we will observe that light is the common theme that makes our physical eyes to function optimally— and same applies to our spiritual eyes! That's why David asked God, "Open thou mine eyes, that I may behold wondrous things out of thy law." (Psalm 119:18). The 'law' being referred to here is the word of God. The word is the light of our harvest; the better our ability to decode the light of the Word, the greater our ability to recognize our harvest.

Do you see it?

God asks us a question in Isaiah 43:19, "I am creating something new. There it is! DO YOU SEE IT? I have put roads in deserts, streams in thirsty lands." (Isaiah 43:19 CEV)

If God is creating your harvest and you cannot see it, that is amplified futility! Of course, naturally, you hardly find roads in the wilderness or rivers in a desert, but what God is doing in that prophetic verse of the scripture is to invite us to behold His miraculous provisions which comprise our harvest. However, it takes a single-eyed individual to see this.

So, what exactly do you see? This is the question God is asking each of us regarding our harvest. If God takes out time to ask us a question even once, we need to pay a close attention. This question, however, was asked no less than eight times through the scriptures! It requires that every fiber of our attention be directed to answering it.

Joseph Olowe

Can you see your harvest?

Two stories in the scriptures come to mind when we think of people who stood by their harvest and yet couldn't recognize it. First is the story of the 12 spies sent to spy the Promised Land (Numbers 13 and 14). They went into their harvest (the Promised Land), but only two of them saw the harvest for what it was; the other 10 didn't see it and as such they roamed for another four decades in the wilderness till the generation of those who couldn't see the harvest perished.

Likewise, the story of Elisha and Gehazi comes to mind. In 2 Kings 6:17, we read: "And Elisha prayed, and said, Lord, I pray thee, open his eyes, that he may see. And the Lord opened the eyes of the young man; and he saw: and, behold, the mountain was full of horses and chariots of fire round about Elisha."

The emphasis here is on that phrase: "The mountain was full..." Isn't it astonishing that very many times, we look and all we see is emptiness (empty bank accounts, empty womb, empty store houses etc). If only our eyes are opened! Then and only then shall we see that where we thought there is an emptiness, there is fullness beyond our imaginations!

CALL TO ACTION

What can you see now? Are you able to recognize your harvest on the field? What do you see? What are you seeing? Emptiness or fullness? Opportunities are sometimes disguised as challenges. Google the story of WALTER CARR; it will give you a contemporary application of what we have learnt in this chapter.

CLOSING THOUGHT

"And Lot lifted up his eyes, and beheld all the plain of Jordan, that it was well watered every where, before the Lord destroyed Sodom and Gomorrah, even as the garden of the Lord, like the land of Egypt, as thou comest unto Zoar. Then Lot chose him all the plain of Jordan; and Lot journeyed east: and they separated themselves the one from the other…For all the land which thou seest, to thee will I give it, and to thy seed for ever" (Genesis 13:10-11).

Abraham chose a dry land while Lot chose the well-watered land to the naked eyes. But in reality, Abraham's inner eyes captured much more—as far as he could see! What do you see? You need your inner eye to see the fullness of your harvest. And did you notice God's choice of words to Abraham? He gave him all the land he could see! In other words, if you cannot see it, then you cannot have it. If you don't want to see it for yourself, please do it for the sake of your seed. What you harvest today is generational not transitional. Shalom.

PRAYER POINTS

1. Father, open the eyes of my heart so that l can see You first.

2. Father, I cry out to you today, please deliver me from every spiritual blindness robbing me of my harvest in the name of Jesus.

3. Help me, Lord, not to miss the time of my harvest in the name of Jesus.

4. Father, my request like that of Bartholomew is that I may see. Open my inner eye, Lord.

5. Father, let my eye see my benefactors when they come around to help me in the name of Jesus.

9
YOUR HARVEST, YOUR HANDS AND YOUR FEET

"But when the grain ripens, immediately he puts in the sickle, because the harvest has come." (Mark 4:29)

Now we are at the home stretch of this wonderful study. What a glorious light God has brought into our lives by showing us the importance of the seedtime and harvest principle. Knowing the inner workings of this principle has been one of the sweetest discoveries I have had since my walk with the Lord began in 1985.

In this book so far, we have unpacked the lessons Jesus taught regarding the various steps of development from seedtime to harvest. First, we have seen that to have a harvest, we must sow and do it right. Thereafter, as we patiently nurture the seed by watering and ensuring that weeds and thorns that can choke it are kept away, the seed gradually develops towards maturation and harvest.

We have extensively and graphically examined this final process of maturation and harvest, which the Lord Himself tells us is divided into three stages. First is the BLADE STAGE, which corresponds with the use of our tongue blade ("a man shall be satisfied by the fruit of his lips…"); second is the EAR STAGE which corresponds with the use of our ear for hearing, by which we develop our faith ("For faith comes by hearing and hearing by the word of the Lord…"); and the third is the FULL CORN STAGE which corresponds with the preparedness of our HEART ("preparations of the heart belong to man, and the answer of the tongue, are from the LORD").

We have also looked at the role of the eye with regards to our ability to see when our harvest is ready. When our eye is single, then we become laser focused on the end result which is a bountiful harvest.

In this concluding chapter, we consider one more thought in our discussions about the preparedness of our heart. We have established that it is with our hearts that we believe. In other words, faith is operational in our heart. But James shows another dimension to us on the subject of faith. He asks us an interesting question:

"What doth it profit, my brethren, though a man say he hath faith, and have not works? Can faith save him?" (James 2:14).

The answer to that is obvious: NO! Faith without works is dead!

In the passage we have explored in this book (Mark 4:3-29), it is apparent that Jesus also mentioned the faith-work balance. It is not enough to have the understanding of how to use our tongue, ears, heart, and eyes so that we can see when our bountiful harvest is ready; the acts of sowing and harvesting, in themselves, require work! We have spent some time to dwell on the work side of sowing (action) in chapter two. Here, we shall consider the work aspect of the harvesting process.

Mark 4:29 says, "... when the fruit is brought forth, immediately he putteth in the sickle, because the harvest is come."

Jesus reveals to here that when the fruit is brought forth, the sower immediately puts in the sickle—that's work! The use of the sickle requires some actions from your end. It involves, amongst other things, the use of two other body parts: your hands and feet. These are the parts of our body that symbolically correspond to works symbolically according to the scriptures. When we engage our hands and feet, the harvest that has come will remain ours; the birds of the air will not be able to devour our harvest by God's grace. So

what are the works that are required of us in this sense? Let us explore the scriptures together.

Seedtime and Harvest

THE REQUIRED WORKS

"I must work the works of him that sent me, while it is day: the night cometh, when no man can work." (John 9:4)

What does it mean to work for your harvest? Before I answer that question, let me point out the fact that this aspect of our harvest is time-bound. Jesus Christ revealed to us in Mark 4:29 that the harvest must be done immediately because a time is coming that we might not be able to do it anymore. Jesus admonishes us in John 9:4 that He himself must work while it is day (in other words, immediately, to reap the harvest of souls) because the night is coming when no man can work. So, what are the works that are needed to facilitate the reaping of our mighty harvest requiring the use of our hands and feet? Praise and Thanksgiving!

To reap the great harvest, we must begin the seedtime with praises and conclude the harvest with thanksgiving. These two expressions of our worship often require us to use our hands and feet. Many scriptures attest to this:

THE USE OF YOUR HANDS

1. "And Solomon stood before the altar of the Lord in the presence of all the congregation of Israel, and spread forth his hands toward heaven: And it was so,

that when Solomon had made an end of praying all this prayer and supplication unto the Lord, he arose from before the altar of the Lord, from kneeling on his knees with his hands spread up to heaven." (1 Kings 8:22, 54)

2. "And Ezra blessed the Lord, the great God. And all the people answered, Amen, Amen, with lifting up their hands: and they bowed their heads, and worshipped the Lord with their faces to the ground." (Nehemiah 8:6)

3. "Lift up your hands in the sanctuary, and bless the Lord." (Psalms 134:2)

4. "O clap your hands, all ye people; shout unto God with the voice of triumph." (Psalms 47:1)

THE USE OF YOUR FEET

We dance with our feet.

1. "Let them praise his name in the dance: let them sing praises unto him with the timbrel and harp. For the Lord taketh pleasure in his people: he will beautify the meek with salvation." (Psalms 149:3-4)

2. "And Miriam the prophetess, the sister of Aaron, took a timbrel in her hand; and all the women went out after her with timbrels and with dances. And Miriam answered them, Sing ye to the Lord, for he

hath triumphed gloriously; the horse and his rider hath he thrown into the sea." (Exodus 15:20-21)

3. "Praise him with the timbrel and dance: praise him with stringed instruments and organs." (Psalms 150:4)

4. "And David danced before the Lord with all his might; and David was girded with a linen ephod." (2 Samuel 6:14)

CALL TO ACTION

Are you doing the work that is required of you? Are you backing up your faith with praise and thanksgiving? When was the last time you praised God with your hands and feet? Begin now to praise Him ,singing, clapping and dancing..

CLOSING THOUGHT

"Although the fig tree shall not blossom, neither shall fruit be in the vines; the labour of the olive shall fail, and the fields shall yield no meat; the flock shall be cut off from the fold, and there shall be no herd in the stalls: Yet I will rejoice in the Lord, I will joy in the God of my salvation." (Habakkuk 3:17-18)

Even if you cannot see anything yet on your field and it seems that you have done everything stated so far in this book, beloved, still rejoice in the Lord! By doing so, the Lord will make your feet like hind's feet to trample upon every barrier and conquer every limitation. Shalom.

PRAYER POINTS

1. Father, I thank you for all you have revealed to me in this book.

2. I thank you, Lord, because things are turning around for good in all areas of my life already.

3. Lord, give me the grace to constantly meditate on the revelations you have given me so far, and strengthen me to put all into practice.

4. Lord, I declare that today marks the beginning of a new dawn of greater dominion, victories, breakthroughs and impacts in every aspect of my life, in Jesus' name.

5. Father, as I see my harvest with the eyes of the spirit, lift up my spirit so that l can praise You with my hands and feet, as well as with my mouth and heart, all the days of my life, in the name of Jesus.

ABOUT THE AUTHOR

Dr. Olalekan Joseph Olowe is a physical therapist by trade and a pastor by calling. Together with his wife, Omolade, they are the Presiding Servants over Kingdom Dominion Ministry International (KDMI) with a ministry base at El Paso, Texas, from where they reach out globally.

A graduate of Rocky Mountain University of Health Professionals, with a transitional Doctorate in Physical Therapy, Joseph is blessed with a physical therapy practice in El Paso, Texas. He's a prolific writer and the author of Rebuilding Your Life; The Capacity of a Man; Kingdom Connection, amongst other books.

He's happily married to Omolade and they are blessed with three children.

www.ingramcontent.com/pod-product-compliance
Lightning Source LLC
LaVergne TN
LVHW051838080426
835512LV00018B/2946